The Begin Era

Westview Replica Editions

The concept of Westview Replica Editions is a response to the continuing crisis in academic and informational publishing. Library budgets for books have been severely curtailed. Ever larger portions of general library budgets are being diverted from the purchase of books and used for data banks, computers, micromedia, and other methods of information retrieval. Interlibrary loan structures further reduce the edition sizes required to satisfy the needs of the scholarly community. Economic pressures on the university presses and the few private scholarly publishing companies have severely limited the capacity of the industry to properly serve the academic and research communities. As a result, many manuscripts dealing with important subjects, often representing the highest level of scholarship, are no longer economically viable publishing projects--or, if accepted for publication, are typically subject to lead times ranging from one to three years.

Westview Replica Editions are our practical solution to the problem. We accept a manuscript in camera-ready form, typed according to our specifications, and move it immediately into the production process. As always, the selection criteria include the importance of the subject, the work's contribution to scholarship, and its insight, originality of thought, and excellence of exposition. The responsibility for editing and proofreading lies with the author or sponsoring institution. We prepare chapter headings and display pages, file for copyright, and obtain Library of Congress Cataloging in Publication Data. A detailed manual contains simple instructions for preparing the final typescript, and our editorial staff is always available to answer questions.

The end result is a book printed on acid-free paper and bound in sturdy library-quality soft covers. We manufacture these books ourselves using equipment that does not require a lengthy make-ready process and that allows us to publish first editions of 300 to 600 copies and to reprint even smaller quantities as needed. Thus, we can produce Replica Editions quickly and can keep even very specialized books in print as long as there is a demand for them.

About the Book and Editor

The Begin Era:
Issues in Contemporary Israel
edited by Steven Heydemann

The years of Menachem Begin's leadership were among the most
turbulent in Israeli history. Domestically, the preeminence of the
Labor Alignment was successfully challenged, the Likud government
failed to reduce Israel's high inflation rate, military and
security expenditures reached new highs, and the politicization
of economic policy increased. Internationally, although Israel's
policy toward the occupied territories and its regional strategy
were the focus of domestic and international debate, Begin's
policies--departures from earlier norms--did successfully define
Israel's foreign policy agenda, and his outlook is likely to continue to influence policy considerations. The contributors to this
volume explore how Israel changed under Begin, the source of those
changes, and how Israel is likely to evolve in a post-Begin era.

Steven Heydemann is director of programs at the Middle East
Institute in Washington, D.C.

Published in cooperation with the
Middle East Institute,
Washington, D.C.

The Begin Era
Issues in Contemporary Israel

edited by
Steven Heydemann

Westview Press / Boulder and London

A Westview Replica Edition

Copyright © 1984 by Westview Press, Inc.

Published in 1984 in the United States of America by
    Westview Press, Inc.
    5500 Central Avenue
    Boulder, Colorado 80301
    Frederick A. Praeger, Publisher

Library of Congress Cataloging in Publication Data
Main entry under title:
The Begin era.
    (A Westview replica edition)
    1. Israel--Politics and government--Addresses, essays, lectures.
2. Begin, Menachem, 1913-   --Addresses, essays, lectures.
I. Heydemann, Steven.
DS126.5.B358   1984   956.94'054   84-19536
ISBN 0-86531-885-9

Printed and bound in the United States of America
10 9 8 7 6 5 4 3 2 1

Contents

Preface

   Menachem Begin's abrupt departure from Israeli
political life marks the end of an era in Israeli
politics. Nonetheless, the debate over Begin's place
in Israel's history and the impact of his policies
continues with undiminished intensity. As some have
noted, his presence loomed larger in the campaign that
preceded the July elections than that of his successor,
Yitzhak Shamir.
   The papers in this volume represent an effort to
confront these issues by assessing the changes and
forces that emerged in Israel during Begin's tenure as
prime minister and their continuing influence in the
period since his leaving office. The papers were presented at a conference held at the Johns Hopkins University School of Advanced International Studies on
January 20, 1984. Much has transpired since these
papers were prepared, but the basic issues they raise
are no closer to a solution today than they were in
January.
   This collection covers three thematic sections:
Israel's foreign and defense policies, political and
ideological trends, and the status of Israel's economy.
In the first section, Bernard Reich evaluates the "special relationship" between the U.S. and Israel, while
Jerrold Green discusses U.S.-Israeli relations in the
broader context of U.S. Middle East policy. Zeev
Schiff's assessment of relations between the government
and the armed forces presents a disturbing view of the
erosion of government control over the actions of the
military.
   In the second section, Gary Schiff reaffirms the
centrality of the religious parties, highlighting the
debate over how to respond to the problems that have
accompanied the expansion of religious politics. Myron
Aronoff explores the reemergence of ideology in Israel
during the Begin era and the weakening of the cohesive
values and perceptions that bind Israelis together. In
his discussion of the West Bank as a factor in Israeli

politics, Ian Lustick concludes that the "point of no return" involves both the physical integration of the West Bank into Israel and the psychological threshold beyond which the majority of Israelis cease to distinguish between the two.

In the third section, David Fand and Kenneth Stammerman both argue that the politicization of economic policy-making has become more pervasive and threatens Israel's economic health in the years ahead. Howard Pack places Israel's economy in a comparative framework to evaluate the country's economic difficulties in relation to those of other nations at a similar stage of development.

In many ways, Israel has not fully emerged from the Begin era. Perhaps more than any other Israeli leader since David Ben-Gurion, Begin has shaped Israel's options and defined issues that Israelis are struggling with today. It is our hope that the following papers represent a small contribution to the understanding and interpretation of that struggle.

Steven Heydemann
July 1984

Acknowledgments

Many people and organizations helped to bring about the conference for which these papers were prepared, and the publication of this collection. Merle Thorpe and the Foundation for Middle East Peace provided important financial support. Hamied Ansari and the Johns Hopkins University School of Advanced International Studies made their facilities available to the Middle East Institute. Melissa Vaughn and the Institute staff deserve credit for their large part in making sure that the conference ran smoothly and for their advice and assistance at every subsequent stage.

Steven Heydemann

1
Israel and the United States: The Special Relationship Reexamined

Bernard Reich

The affinity of the United States and Israel antedates Israel's independence in 1948. Support for the idea of a Jewish state developed after World War I and concrete efforts to achieve the goal began to appear in United States policy discussions soon after World War II. Israel was a creation of the United Nations, but the United States has been its main benefactor, particularly since 1967, and today is essential to ensure Israel's future.

Between 1947 and 1977 the United States and Israel developed a complex relationship, which fluctuated between relative indifference and closeness, and developed from an essentially humanitarian focus to a multifaceted relationship. At the outset the United States based its policy on the humanitarian considerations associated with the plight of European Jewry, but by the 1970s political and strategic considerations were dominant. United States policy on arms supply evolved from "embargo" to "principal supplier," and arms became an important tool of United States policy to reassure Israel and to achieve policy modifications. The two states developed a diplomatic-political relationship that focused on the need to resolve the Arab-Israeli dispute. But while they agreed on the general concept, they often differed on the precise means of achieving the desired result.

The relationship became especially close after the June War of 1967. A congruence of policy prevailed on many of the salient concerns of the two states, and a certain exclusivity seemed to develop in United States Middle East policy. However, despite general concord there were also significant disputes. The two states often held differing perspectives on regional developments, on their dangers and opportunities, and on the appropriate form of response. No major ruptures took place, although significant tensions were generated at various junctures, such as during the Suez crisis of 1956-57.

1

The accession to office of Jimmy Carter in Washington and of Menachem Begin in Jerusalem in 1977 inaugurated a new period in the relationship, characterized by increased public tension and, sometimes, recrimination. Carter and Begin focused on the Arab-Israeli peace process and the desire to terminate the conflict. Nevertheless they often disagreed on the modalities and the interim objectives of the peace process and there were significant personality clashes between senior American and Israeli figures. There was also a reduced exclusivity in the relationship, especially after the Sadat visit to Jerusalem in November 1977.

The record of the first three years of the Reagan administration was a mixed one. There were periods of discord and others reflecting policy congruence. The two states clashed over divergent interpretations of the regional situation, of the peace process, and of Israel's security requirements. The war in Lebanon and associated developments raised significant questions about various aspects of their links. However, a number of events contributed to the improvement of United States-Israel relations in 1982-1983: King Hussein failed to join the peace process in the wake of the Reagan initiative of September 1982, Soviet involvement in Syria increased significantly, and Israel and Lebanon reached an accord (although later aborted), under United States auspices. By early 1984 the two nations seemed linked by a congruence of policy that included recognition of Israel's strategic anti-Soviet value and its desire for peaceful resolution of the Arab-Israeli conflict. This comported with President Reagan's initial perceptions of Israel and presaged a period of positive relations between the United States and Israel. The absence of a peace process and the expected elections in Israel and the United States suggested that the positive links between the two nations would prevail for the remainder of the Reagan administration's initial term in office.

The U.S. National Interest and the Israel Component

The United States national interest lies in its continued independent existence, survival and security with its institutions and values safeguarded, and with the welfare of its people enhanced. There is an "American ideology" that seeks democratic institutions, with morality and principles as guidelines of policy, and with liberty and human rights for its own people and for others. "Making the world safe for democracy" is an operational imperative. The United States cannot

maintain its existence in isolation; it requires a
world conducive to its unique political experiment.
   In the Middle East, United States interests and
concerns can be cataloged with substantial agreement
although debate surrounds their priority. Preventing
Soviet dominance (and the expansion of its power and
influence in the area); assuring the flow of oil at
reasonable prices, particularly to American friends and
allies; assuring access to regional markets as a means
of recycling the petrodollars earned by the regional
states through the sale of oil; and the security and
well-being of Israel are at the core.[1] The United
States has increasingly seen it as "in its interest" to
resolve the Arab-Israeli conflict.
   There is general agreement that Israel is an important interest and has achieved a special position
accorded to no other state in the Middle East, despite
some disagreement as to whether or not this should be
the case. Recognition of the interest is widespread
and essentially beyond the realm of debate, even by
observers such as George Ball who are regarded by Israel as hostile to it:

   First of all, one of our interests in the Middle
   East is the carrying out of a rather deep emotional commitment to the Israeli people to permit them
   to achieve their objective of a national home.
   Now this goes back a long way.... From a strictly
   strategic position, apart from the intellectual
   and emotional basis for our commitment, the fact
   that we had made it not formally and in treaty
   form, but in a dozen different ways, means that we
   should sustain it. It is not in the American interest to engage in a reversal of alliances, or to
   indicate that we abandon our friends. Israel is
   established as a friend of the United States.[2]

   There is an ideological concern and a political-
strategic value in the relationship. Israel is seen as
a like-image state whose survival is crucial to the
ideological prospering of the United States. This perspective goes beyond the more general concern for all
similar states to one associated particularly with
Israel:

   It is unthinkable that the international community
   could stand idly by ... if Israel were in danger
   of destruction. The moral and political convul-
   sion which such an event would engender is beyond
   calculation. It could spell the end not only of
   the Atlantic alliance, but of liberal civilization
   as we know it.[3]

4

The ideological/emotional interest is buttressed
by a perspective which regards Israel as a political-
strategic asset. As Minority Leader of the House
Gerald Ford said in 1969: "I firmly believe that the
fate of Israel is linked to the national security interests of the United States."[4] Israel has been supportive of United States policy in the United Nations
and in other world forums. Tangible national security
advantages have included the view that Israel is a reliable bulwark against Soviet penetration and domina-
tion of the Middle East and against radical Arab expansion. The Reagan administration codified this perspective in the Memorandum of Understanding on Strategic
Cooperation (1981), which focused on the Soviet threat,
and has articulated this view in the statements of Secretary of Defense Weinberger and other administration
officials.[5]

Israel's strategic value became a component of
American interests primarily after 1967 when specific
contributions could be identified. Israel's positions
in Sinai and along the Suez Canal prevented Soviet use
of the Canal to shorten its supply lines to the Indian
Ocean and Southeast Asia. Israel provided the United
States with valuable military information and intelligence as captured Soviet equipment facilitated United
States countermeasures against similar weaponry in
Vietnam and Israeli experience with American equipment
helped in the modification of designs and tactics.
Israeli military installations could prove valuable to
the United States in various military situations. During the 1970 civil war in Jordan, Israel took actions
which the United States could not because of political
and military constraints. It acted on behalf of the
United States in support of King Hussein to prevent
Syrian intervention on behalf of the PLO. Israel's
highly visible military activities became an element in
United States policy.

President Reagan has articulated his perspective
of Israel's value:

...our own position would be weaker without the
political and military assets Israel provides....
The fall of Iran has increased Israel's value as
perhaps the only remaining strategic asset in the
region on which the United States can truly rely.... Israel has the democratic will, national
cohesion, technological capacity and military
fiber to stand forth as America's trusted ally.[6]

Commentators have argued that American interests;
peace, stability and security in the Middle East, can
be preserved by a strong Israel supported by United
States military and economic assistance, as well as
diplomatic and political support. In this view Israel

represents a solid Western foothold in the region and
serves as a countervailing factor to the Soviet presence in some Arab states.

American credibility is at stake. Israel is perceived by the Arab world and much of the international
community as benefitting from a United States security
commitment. American actions that might be interpreted
as backing away from that obligation would undermine
the credibility of the United States as an ally. If
the United States were to "abandon" Israel, the American role in other, and lesser, relationships would be
open to question.

The United States Component of
Israel's National Interest

Upon independence Israel sought positive relations
with both the United States and the Soviet Union. Although there were strong factors propelling Israel in a
westerly direction, superpower support for the establishment of the Jewish state and an apparent competition between them for closer links with it, suggested
that avoidance of a choice might be possible. This
initial policy of nonalignment (nonidentification)
faded as the Soviet and American perceptions of and
positions in, the Middle East were altered. Almost
inexorably Israel moved into a position of alignment
with the West and estrangement from the East and into a
clear linkage with the United States. This shift to
the West led, by the late 1960s, to the United States
becoming the single most significant element in Israeli
foreign policy. By the late 1970s the United States
had assumed an unrivaled position in the national interest calculations of Israel and had become virtually
indispensable as a source of economic and military assistance as well as political and diplomatic support.

The Domestic American Factor in
United States-Israel Relations

The United States-Israel relationship is a product
of the American decision-making process which, in turn,
is influenced by domestic political factors--public
opinion, political participation, and voting behavior
all have an effect.

The Israel lobby, which seeks to maintain and en-
hance the United States relationship, enjoys a number
of advantages in its efforts to secure its objectives,
including an environment that is generally sympathetic.
Hyman H. Bookbinder, the Washington Representative of
the American Jewish Committee and an important member

of the Israel lobby, has described it succinctly in
these terms:

> The greatest single thing going for American sup-
> port for Israel is the fact that our American
> leaders--the President, Cabinet officials, Sena-
> tors, Congressmen, national security advisers--
> have for 30 years consistently <u>said</u> it is in
> America's interest. I do not contend that the
> great majority of Americans have themselves
> studied this issue carefully, know where the West
> Bank is, [or have] come to their own conclusion.
> They have accepted a national verdict. That ver-
> dict has been that Israel's security is in Ameri-
> ca's interest.[7]

A widespread fund of goodwill toward Israel, not restricted to the Jewish community, favored the establishment and consolidation of a Jewish state in Palestine and favors the continued existence, integrity, and
security of Israel. At the same time pro-Arab forces
have to operate in an environment that provides very
little mass support.

Underlying much of the support is an American perception which sees Israel as the type of state with a
similarity of outlook and generally progressive nature,
which the United States would like to see exist world-
wide. President Gerald Ford, in a White House toast
for Prime Minister Yitzhak Rabin in September 1974,
noted:

> The American people have a great deal of under-
> standing and sympathy and dedication to the same
> kind of ideals that are representative of Israel.
> And, therefore, I think we in America have a cer-
> tain rapport and understanding with the people of
> Israel.... We have mutual aims and objectives.
> We have the kind of relationship that I think, if
> expanded worldwide, would be beneficial to all
> mankind.[8]

In a similar vein, former Israeli Foreign Minister Abba
Eban has identified a "Harmony in democratic values,
harmony of historic roots, harmony in spiritual memories, harmony of ideals, and, I am convinced, a profound, underlying harmony of interests in this hard and
dangerous world."[9]

There is an element of cultural identity that sees
Israel as a "Western" state in a sea of feudal, oriental entities and as a perpetuator of the Judeo-
Christian heritage. It is perceived as sharing the
concept of individual freedom and the right of all individuals to live in peace. It is characterized as a
valiant, young state, which provides a model of courage
and tenacity. Its people have been praised for their

sacrifice, dedication and spirit. Israel is seen as
having achieved substantial progress, despite its pre-
carious existence, and is worthy of emulation. There
is a historical affinity and similarity of national
experience, which includes the immigrant and pioneering
nature of the two states and their respective commitments to democracy. The American experience in striving to escape persecution and establish an independent
national homeland has a parallel in a Jewish state in
Palestine which appears to reaffirm these ideals
through absorption and integration of immigrants in
distress. There has been a corresponding dedication to
the values of pioneering--the United States placed a
premium on the pioneers who heeded the call to "go
west," and Israel places a similar value on the settlers who moved to the frontiers to develop those
areas.

There is a general understanding of Jewish history
and the advantages of the Biblical connection. Israel
fits into the historical-religious collective memory of
Americans.

The relationship is also influenced by the religious perception that Israel is fulfilling the biblical
prophecy that the Jews would return to the promised
land. This perception, nurtured in America's Bible-
belt fundamentalist Christian areas, is further rein-
forced by "Sunday-school stories" linking the Jews to
the Holy Land. In response to the historical persecution of the Jews, particularly the Holocaust and the
destruction of large segments of world Jewry in Europe
in World War II, there was an effort to save the remnant of world Jewry through the maintenance of a sanc-
tuary, which also helped to assuage a "guilt element."
There is also the feeling of moral responsibility de-
riving from the American involvement in the creation of
the state in 1947 and 1948 and from the commitment to
the Balfour Declaration after World War I, the latter
playing a role in Truman's decision to support and
recognize the creation of Israel. There is also the
sympathy that derived from the "underdog" image that
Israel had in relation to the Arab states during much
of the early decades of the Arab-Israeli conflict.

This positive perception of Israel has been complemented by a generally negative image of the Arabs,
although there has been some modification of this image
in recent years, particularly with regard to Sadat and
Egypt.

These perceptions of Israel have been manifest in
the positive views of American public opinion for Israel. Informed Americans have consistently been far more
willing to declare support and sympathy for Israel than
for the Arab states and continue to endorse Israel's
existence, integrity, and security. This also has been

reflected in views on issues of specific concern to
Israel.

In general, sympathy for Israel has remained fairly constant over time although there was an increase
during and immediately after the 1967 and 1973 wars
and in reaction to the completion of the Israeli withdrawal from Sinai in April 1982. The 1982 war in Lebanon showed a different trend. Polls taken soon after
the start of hostilities in June showed that pro-Israel
sympathies were unchanged and Americans appeared to be
somewhat sympathetic to the Israeli incursion, despite
disapproval of specific actions. The massacre at
Shatila and Sabra and related developments in September, seem to have had a significant effect as many
American appeared to hold Israel at least partially
responsible for those events. A poll conducted by Gal-
lup and reported in Newsweek on October 4, 1982 showed
that American sympathies were about evenly divided between Israel and the Arab states. This was the first
time ever that Israel was not heavily favored and much
of the change seemed to be related to the massacres.
Nevertheless, the fundamental, long-standing American
sympathy for and support of Israel has not diminished.
Specific events have caused changes, generally transitory, in popular opinion of Israel or of its policies
or leaders, but apparently have not affected the base
of support. Thus, after the 1977 election which
brought Menachem Begin to power there began to appear a
distinction between support for Israel, on the one
hand, and for the policies and government of Israel, on
the other. Specific disppointments with Begin's policies were not translated into lack of sympathy for
Israel.

The media have also played an important role. In
general, the American media widely reports news concerning Israel and, over the years, has portrayed a
positive (sometimes very positive) image of Israel,
although there has been some modification in recent
years.[10] Editorials have tended to favor Israel over
the Arabs and to support Israel, particularly in the
elite press.[11] Despite the increased coverage of the
Arab world since the 1973 war and the accompanying oil
crisis, the orientation toward, and overall positive
image of, Israel continues. This has tended to rein-
force existing perspectives and proclivities, is reflected in public opinion, and has been instrumental in
Israel's efforts to retain Congressional support.

The Congress continues to be an important element
of support for Israel as indicated in numerous resolutions, votes, statements, cosponsors on resolutions,
public statements, letters for public release, and
other factors. Generally, resolutions and statements
favorable to Israel have had substantial numbers of
cosponsors. On issues of importance, positions

favorable to Israel have been consistently successful in the House and the Senate, although voting support has varied over time and with the specific issue at hand. The support is widespread, and not confined to representatives coming from Jewish population centers-- it includes Republicans and Democrats, conservatives and liberals, although the reasons for support vary from individual to individual, from group to group, and from issue to issue. Pro-Israel strength in the Congress has been such that the administration has utilized it to assist in securing passage of other legislation. Aid for Greece in the days of the junta was argued on the grounds that support of Israel required facilities in Greece and aid to Cambodia was combined with legislation providing aid to Israel in order to facilitate Congressional approval.

Economic and military assistance has been a barometer of Congressional support. Israel has been the beneficiary of significant Congressional efforts to increase its levels of aid. Other actions favoring Israel have included lenient repayment terms and the conversion of loans to grants. Congress initiated new foreign aid programs to Israel's benefit, such as providing funds for the resettlement of Soviet Jews in Israel. Congress has also earmarked specific funds to reduce administration discretion and has included prohibitions in the aid bills to prevent assistance to others that might prove harmful to Israel. Beyond the aid programs themselves Congress has often used legislative measures and other, more indirect, means to influence administration policy in Israel's behalf. Thus, there have been letters and statements and "sense of Congress" resolutions as well as Committee hearings and reports designed to influence the administration and the public.

Support for Israel has also been reflected in careful scrutiny of Arab states appropriations which are sometimes reduced and often granted with conditions. Military sales to the Arab states have been subjected to substantial discussion and often approved only following significant and sometimes embarrassing debate--such as the AWACS decision in 1981. The Congress has passed legislation governing businesses and their compliance with the Arab boycott of Israel and their compliance with various racial and religious restrictions on the employment of Americans in projects in or with the Arab world.

There is a widespread view that Israel's success with the Congress, and with the executive branch, over an extended period is a function of its success in the American political system which, in turn, is attributed to Jewish politicians, Jewish votes and Jewish money. Generally, observers have exaggerated the role and effect of each of these factors. Jews have not been very

disproportionately represented among senior elected officials of the United States. The "Jewish vote" has
been attributed to the concentration of the American
Jewish community in the northeastern states, especially
in those with large blocs of electoral votes which
could be critical in determining the outcome of close
presidential elections. This is significant since Jews
tend to be politically active, thus gaining something
of a multiplier effect for their votes and exerting an
influence out of proportion to their numbers. The
"Jewish vote" tends to have an influence--whether in
reality, when it is actually cast, or in perception,
when the office seeker modifies or tailors his position
to gain or maintain the identified "vote." Jewish money is often regarded as a potent factor in the effort
to gain influence. Jews have been among the important
financial backers of prominent political candidates,
especially Democrats, and among the fund-raisers of the
major parties. Although this factor has been modified
in recent years as a result of campaign reforms, Jewish
donations to political causes have been out of proportion to population percentages and to wealth.

The American Jewish community plays an important
role in the relationship between the United States and
Israel: it seeks to influence policy and to create a
bridge between the Jewish communities of Israel and the
United States and to extend it to the broader American
society. By numerous connections, ranging from tourism
to philanthropy, the link has been established and
maintained.

The Israel-oriented American Jewish organizations
engage in fundraising and education, public relations
and political activity. American Jewry has materially
aided the establishment, development, and consolidation
of Israel through outright philanthropic gifts (primarily through the United Jewish Appeal and the United
Israel Appeal) and the purchase of Israel bonds. There
are also substantial contributions which go directly to
specific charities or programs in Israel, such as hos-
pitals, schools and research institutions. The political and public relations activities have been extensive
and have involved the American Jewish community in cultural, social, educational, public relations, and
political activities on behalf of Israel in the United
States.

The American Jewish community is well organized
and highly structured. It is also highly complex, and
not monolithic or hierarchical. No one organization or
individual represents American Jewry despite the claim
of several to do so. When the issue is Israel-
oriented, the American Israel Public Affairs Committee
(AIPAC) and the Conference of Presidents of Major
American Jewish Organizations (the Conference) are at
the focal point although other organizations, such as

the American Jewish Committee, often pursue their own
course. AIPAC is the only officially registered lobbying organization established for the purpose of influencing legislation on Capitol Hill to improve United
States-Israel relations. It is registered under the
lobbying law and its officially stated purpose is to
maintain and improve the friendship and goodwill between the United States and Israel. The Conference is
a coordinating body of various major Jewish organizations with diverse concerns--fraternal matters, community relations, religious themes, philanthropic activity, and Zionist issues. Originally created in 1955
to present a consensus perspective of the major American Jewish organizations, and to prevent the overlapping of response on matters affecting Israel, it had a
minor role until the June War. With the "Zionization"
of the American Jewish community in 1967, with the
growing links between the communities, and with the increased need for coordination of the various groups,
the Conference became a mechanism for contact and con-
sultation between Israel and American Jewry at the most
senior levels. The Conference concentrates its activities in the executive branch, much as AIPAC devotes its
primary efforts to the legislative branch.
     The precise role and success of the Jewish com-
munity and Israel interest group in influencing the
nature of United States policy toward Israel is impossible to measure, but it is clear that ties with Israel
partly reflect the efforts of these groups and individual Jewish leaders. Although no precise judgment is
possible, the success and failure of the Israel lobby
has been highlighted by events in recent years: the
1975 letter from 76 Senators to President Ford endors-
ing aid to Israel, and the 1978 and 1981 votes permitting the sale of F-15 jets and AWACS, respectively, to
Saudi Arabia. The former was an important achievement,
the latter debatable "failures." United States military and economic aid has been the most tangible accomplishment.
     American Jewish supporters of Israel, and Israel
itself, have long realized the need for Christian support. The ability of pro-Israel groups to form coalitions with other domestic elements and to secure en-
dorsements from such diverse sources as prominent public figures, Black leaders, scholars, entertainers,
etc., has been a positive element.
     The American religious heritage, overwhelmingly
Christian, helps to secure a religious interest in and
link to the land and people of Israel. Father Robert
Drinan has described it in these terms:

     There is...a profound bond between the Christians
     of America and the Jews of Israel. This bond goes
     back to the fact that the original pilgrims who

came to America from Europe did so because they
were persecuted for religious or political reasons
in their fatherland. Because of the similarity of
the origin of immigration to Israel, Christians in
America have a profound, if unconscious, affinity
for the hundreds of thousands of Jews who have
gone to Israel since the holocaust.[12]

Christian support for Israel has varied in intensity since the debates in the 1940s over the creation
of the Jewish state. Traditional and mainstream Christian groups have provided support over an extended period, although in recent years the evangelical movement
has become increasingly significant. Within the American Christian community "...the most influential and
vocal elements of the Religious Right [evangelical and
fundamentalist Christians, estimated at betwen thirty
to fifty million] are the greatest champions of Israel
outside the Jewish community itself."[13] The basis for
this strong pro-Israel perspective lies in their approach to the Bible.

According to their interpretation of scripture, it
is essential that the Jews be re-gathered in the
Holy Land before Christ will come again. Only
after the establishment of a new Israeli nation
can the drama of the "end days" begin. It com-
mences with a seven-year period of great tribula-
tions, during which the anti-Christ temporarily
rules the world and ends with the catastrophic
Battle of Armaggedon (in Israel). Before human-
kind completely destroys itself in this bloody
battle, Christ returns to save the faithful Bible
believers and to usher in the millennium.[14]

Given this perspective, Israel's establishment provided
"proof" that biblical prophecies were being fulfilled.

The Nature of the Commitment

In a press conference on May 12, 1977, President
Jimmy Carter said:

We have a special relationship with Israel. It's
absolutely crucial that no one in our country or
around the world ever doubt that our No. 1 commitment in the Middle East is to protect the right of
Israel to exist, to exist permanently, and to exist in peace. It's a special relationship.[15]

Israel's special relationship with the United
States, based on substantial positive perception and
sentiment evident in public opinion and official

statements and manifest in political-diplomatic support
and military and economic assistance, has not been en-
shrined in a legally binding commitment joining the two
states in a formal alliance. Despite the substantial
links which have developed, the widespread belief in
the existence of the commitment, and the assurances
contained in various specific agreements such as Sinai
II and the letters attached to the Camp David accords
and the Egypt-Israel Peace Treaty, the exact nature and
extent of the United States commitment to Israel remains imprecise.

Israel has no mutual security treaty with the
United States, nor is it a member of any alliance system requiring the United States to take up arms automatically on its behalf. It has been assumed that the
United States would come to Israel's assistance should
it be gravely threatened and this perception has become
particularly apparent during times of crisis. Despite
this perception and the general "feeling" in Washington
and elsewhere that the United States would take action
if required, there is no assurance that this would be
the case. The exact role of the United States in support of Israel, beyond diplomatic and political action
and military and economic assistance, is unclear.

The commitment has taken the rather generalized
form of Presidential statements rather than formal
documents. American statements of policy have reaf-
firmed American interest and concern in supporting the
political independence and territorial integrity of
Middle Eastern states, including Israel. They do not,
however, commit the United States to specific actions
in particular circumstances.

In April 1969 the Senate Foreign Relations Committee summarized the United States commitment to Israel
in these terms:

> Consider, for example, the widely held view that
> the United States is committed to the defense of
> Israel even though we have no security treaty with
> that country. The source of this alleged commit-
> ment is in fact nothing more than a long series of
> executive policy declarations, including: Presi-
> dent Truman's declaration of support for the in-
> dependence of Israel in 1948; the British-French-
> American tripartite declaration of 1950 pledging
> opposition to the violation of frontiers or armi-
> stice lines in the Middle East; President Eisen-
> hower's statement of January 1957 pledging Ameri-
> can support for the integrity and independence of
> Middle Eastern Nations; Secretary of State Dul-
> les' assertion of February 1957 that the United
> States regarded the Gulf of Aqaba as an interna-
> tional waterway; President Kennedy's press

conference of March 1963 pledging American opposition to any act of aggression in the Middle East;
and President Johnson's statements of February
1964 indicating American support for the territorial integrity and political independence of all
Middle Eastern countries.

All of these declarations are executive policy
statements; not one is based on a treaty ratified
by the Senate. The only treaty commitment the
United States has in the Middle East is as a sig-
natory to the United Nations Charter.... It is
not the committee's position that the United
States ought not to come to the support of Israel
should it be the victim of aggression. It is the
committee's position that, should so significant
an obligation be incurred, it ought to be the result of a treaty or other appropriate legislative
instrumentality.[16]

In more recent years, the arrangement has been
codified in the Sinai II accords of 1975 and the Memorandum of Understanding on Strategic Cooperation of
1981, although commitments made in the Egypt-Israel
peace process and other "memoranda" have been significant. But, despite the Sinai II assurance, they did
not provide a formal and legally binding commitment for
United States military action.

Israeli leaders continue to be interested in military and economic assistance as the primary tangible
expression of the American commitment and have been
particularly cautious about potential United States
participation in conflict--they do not want Americans
fighting in or for Israel. They are concerned about
possible Vietnam-analogous situations and see this in
the American debate in 1983 and 1984 concerning Central
America.

Although the United States has incurred no legally
binding commitment requiring it to come to Israel's assistance in the event of conflict, it is clear that
there is general support for the commitment to Israel.
This tends to render a formal document superfluous and
perhaps undesirable. The critical factor is not the
formal requirement but the perception of it and the
willingness to act in support of perceived obligations.
In the final analysis the commitment of the United
States to Israel will reflect the nature of the relationship at any particular time.

The Future of the Relationship:
Consensus and Discord

Over nearly four decades the United States and Israel have established a special relationship replete

with broad areas of agreement and numerous examples of discord. The two states have worked together in many spheres. Broad agreement and understanding and a generalized commitment to peace exists, and specific questions and issues have been consistently approached within that framework. It is with regard to the specifics, especially the tactics and techniques to be employed in efforts to achieve the broad objectives, that the relationship has had its episodes of disagreement. Agreement on broad goals and discord on specifics is likely to characterize their relationship in the future.

The two states maintain a remarkable degree of parallelism and congruence on broad policy goals. The policy consensus includes the need to prevent war, both regional and global, the need to resolve the Arab-Israeli conflict, and the need to maintain Israel's existence and security and to help provide for its economic well-being. At the same time there was, is, and will be, a divergence that derives from a difference of perspective and overall policy environment. The United States has broader concerns resulting from its global obligations, while Israel's perspective is conditioned by its more restricted environment and lesser responsibilities. Israel's horizon is more narrowly defined and essentially limited to the survival of the state and a concern for Jewish communities and individuals which goes beyond the frontiers of the Jewish state.

There has been a divergence on methods and techniques to be employed as well as discord on specific issues, including the appropriate form of response to Arab terrorism, the value of great power efforts to resolve the Arab-Israeli conflict, the appropriateness and timing of face-to-face and direct Arab-Israeli negotiations, and the provision of essential military supplies (types, quantities, and timing).

In many respects the issue of Jerusalem has highlighted the areas of discord. The United States has supported the Partition Plan designation of Jerusalem as a separate entity and has stressed the international character of the city while refusing to recognize unilateral actions by any state affecting its future. The United States refuses to move its embasssy to Jerusalem and maintains it in Tel Aviv, thus illustrating the differing perspectives of the two states. These perspectives have placed the two states in conflicting positions virtually continuously from 1947 to the present, especially since the Israeli declarations of Jerusalem as the capital of the state and the reunification of the city during the 1967 war.

The two states will continue to hold divergent views on the several elements of the Palestinian issue, particularly the West Bank's future, the rights of the Palestinians, and the potential creation of a

Palestinian homeland, entity or state. These differences have become increasingly obvious in the Carter
and Reagan administrations, particularly during the
course of the autonomy negotiations. They have differed over the construction of settlements in the territories and whether they are legal and/or obstacles to
peace.

There have been personality clashes. Senior
American and Israeli officials have not always been
compatible and this has affected the tenor of the relationship. This was particularly evident in the relations between Carter and Begin. In the Reagan administration mutual dislike and mistrust extended further--
the United States was unhappy with Prime Minister Menachem Begin and Defense Minister Ariel Sharon while Israel had strong anxieties about Secretary of Defense
Caspar Weinberger and his policies.

There have been disagreements concerning the nature of the situation in the region, often focusing on
alternative intelligence estimates of the threat.

In an interview in 1969 then Prime Minister Golda
Meir summarized the situation in these terms:

> We have been very fortunate that there is a basic
> friendship to Israel and this doesn't change with
> the administration. There have been problems at
> various times since the state of Israel was estab-
> lished, and every once in a while we don't see eye
> to eye as to how the problem should be solved.
> But underlying these differences of opinion there
> is always the consciousness we carry with us that
> basically there is a deep friendship, understand-
> ing, and concern for the existence of Israel.[17]

The general consensus on major issues does not ensure
agreement on all aspects or specifics of each problem.
As the dialogue has increasingly dealt with details,
rather than broad areas of agreement, there have been
disturbances in the relationship. Israel and the
United States understand that this is inevitable, but
seek to minimize the areas of discord. Strains in the
relationship are probably inevitable given the extensive nature of the issues that will be considered in
the dialogue.

Yitzhak Shamir described the situation in these
terms to the Knesset:

> Our relations with the United States are of a spe-
> cial character. Between our two nations there is
> a deep friendship, based on common values and
> identical interests. At the same time, differ-
> ences between our two countries crop up occasion-
> ally, chiefly on the subject of our borders and
> how to defend our security. These differences of

opinion are natural; they stem from changing conditions, and they express our independence and our
separate needs.... Israel is a difficult ally,
but a faithful and reliable one. We are certain
that what we have in common with the United States
is permanent and deep, while our disagreements are
ephemeral. The permanent will overcome the
ephemeral.[18]

There are limits on the relationship, concerning
the goals to be sought and the methods to achieve them,
beyond which neither side will go. The United States
will not push Israel beyond certain parameters and Israel will not risk losing American support by refusing
to respond when essential. Yitzhak Shamir commented:

...on the fundamental life-and-death issues--such
as security, Jerusalem, the 1967 borders, the
danger of a Palestinian state--we have no choice
but to stand by our position firmly, strongly and
clearly--even against our great friend the United
States.[19]

Prospects

1984 is likely to be a year of tranquility in the
United States-Israel relationship. A major element in
assuring this period of concord is the elections in Israel in July and the United States in November.
Neither American nor Israeli leaders wish to enter an
election season with a cloud over the ties between
these two nations. There are, in addition, other factors which will contribute to the positive nature of
the links. There are no negotiations concerning peace
in the Middle East and thus no forum for the airing of
the considerable differences between the two states on
the modalities and issues of the peace process. Second, there is a general congruence between them on the
interpretation of the political and strategic situation
in the region and the identification of the positive
and negative forces acting therein. Thus on procedural
and substantive grounds there is little base for discord between the parties. The issues have not been
eliminated nor even covered up, they are simply not "on
the agenda" for the type of discussion which might promote public discord.
The quadrennial American presidential election
season is characterized by a hiatus in the peace process and a positive aura for the special relationship.
This mimics past patterns but also reflects the reality
of the situation in 1984 when there was no clear and
obvious mechanism for a breakthrough in the peace
process. But the process will resume, given its

18

centrality to both the United States and Israel, and
the issues will be contentious, given the positions of
the parties. Periodic crises will emerge and there
will be clashes between the United States and Israel
that will, no doubt, be characterized, as their predecessors have been, as "the worst ever."   Observers
are continually predicting "inevitable collisions" and
"confrontations" in the relationship. However, given
the strong ties linking the United States and Israel in
the special relationship, the storms of the future will
be weathered as have those of the past. The relationship has survived the poor personal relations of Carter
and Begin, and, as seen by Israel, the Weinberger on-
slaught, as well as significant substantive disagreements such as those surrounding the war in Lebanon, the
AWACS debate, the Reagan initiative, and the Sabra-
Shatila massacres.   Its resilience is noteworthy and
likely to be maintained. Zbigniew Brzezinski has identified many of the reasons for it in this observation:

> The relationship between the United States and Is-
> rael is genuinely organic and moral in character.
> I put that above any formal ties of alliance or
> treaties. There are such direct personal links
> between America and Israel, and there is such a
> sense of moral identification with Israel because
> of what has happened in the last 40 years that
> this relationship is as strong as ever and as en-
> during as ever.[20]

The special relationship will continue with its
particular patterns unique to the links between the
United States and Israel.

NOTES

1. On United States interests in the Middle East
see Bernard Reich, "United States Interests in the Middle East," in Haim Shaked and Itamar Rabinovich, eds.,
The Middle East and the United States: Perceptions and
Policies (New Brunswick and London: Transaction Books,
1980), pp. 53-92 and Seth P. Tillman, The United States
in the Middle East: Interests and Obstacles (Blooming-
ton: Indiana University Press, 1982).
2. "American Policy on Trial: An Interview with
George Ball," Journal of Palestine Studies Vol. 7
(Spring 1978), p. 20. See also George W. Ball, "How to
Save Israel in Spite of Herself," Foreign Affairs
Vol. 55 (April 1977), 453-471.
3. Eugene V. Rostow, "The American Stake in Israel," Commentary Vol. 63 (April 1977), p. 46.

4. _National Jewish Monthly_, June 1969, pp. 10 and 12.

5. In a speech on May 13, 1983 Weinberger said that the Soviet Union was actively seeking to undermine moderate and Western-oriented regimes in the Middle East and that its military power posed a grave threat to American interests in the region. "We know that the Soviets would dearly love control over the Middle East's resources and strategic chokepoints, but Israel stands determinedly in their way."

6. Ronald Reagan, "Recognizing the Israeli Asset," _Washington Post_, August 15, 1979. During the campaign for the presidency Reagan said, in a speech to B'nai B'rith on September 3, 1980: "...the touchstone of our relationship with Israel is that a secure, strong Israel is in America's self-interest. Israel is a major strategic asset to America."

7. William J. Lanouette, "The Many Faces of the Jewish Lobby in America," _National Journal_, Vol. 10 (May 13, 1978), p. 749.

8. White House Press Release, September 12, 1974.

9. Abba Eban, _Near East Report_, April 23, 1975, p. 72.

10. See William C. Adams, ed., _Television Coverage of the Middle East_ (Norwood, New Jersey: ABLEX Publishing Corporation, 1981), especially chapters 1, 4 and 5.

11. See S. Robert Lichter, "Media Support for Israel: A Survey of Leading Journalists," in William C. Adams, ed., _Television Coverage of the Middle East_ (Norwood, New Jersey: ABLEX Publishing Corporation, 1981), 40-52. Robert H. Trice, "The American Elite Press and the Arab-Israeli Conflict," _Middle East Journal_ Vol. 33 (Summer 1979), 304-325 explores the role of the elite press in the period from 1966 to 1974.

12. Robert F. Drinan, _Honor the Promise: America's Commitment to Israel_ (Garden City, New York: Doubleday and Company, Inc., 1977), p. 3.

13. Ruth W. Mouly, "Israel: Darling of the Religious Right," _The Humanist_ Vol. 42 (May/June 1982), p. 6.

14. _Ibid_.

15. _New York Times_, May 13, 1977.

16. United States Senate, Committee on Foreign Relations _Report_, _National Commitments_, 91st Congress, 1st Session, April 16, 1969, pp. 26-27.

17. Interview in _U.S. News and World Report_, September 22, 1969, p. 54.

18. Shamir speech to the Knesset, September 8, 1982.

19. _Ibid_.

20. "The World According to Brzezinski," James Reston interview with Zbigniew Brzezinski, _New York Times Magazine_, December 31, 1978, p. 11.

2
America and the Middle East in the Post-Begin Era

Jerrold D. Green

Introduction

Pundits at the time of Anwar Sadat's assassination wryly noted that Sadat had lost two elections; one in America where Ronald Reagan was elected and the other in Israel in which Menachem Begin was reelected. In terms of the turbulent realities of Middle East politics Reagan's ascent certainly heralded far greater changes than Begin's retirement. Certainly the post-Begin era in Israel has led to significant changes, but these have been primarily in the domain of domestic economic policy.[1] In the foreign policy realm, at least to date, Prime Minister Yitzhak Shamir has taken pains to cloak himself in the mantle of his predecessor. Thus, for those concerned with developments in the Middle East, the post-Carter era serves as a far more significant analytical watershed than the post-Begin era. It is the policy of the Reagan administration, both towards Israel and the Middle East in general, which is the focus of this paper.[2]
Analysts of all political persuasions have been extremely critical of the Reagan administration's foreign policy record. There are many who argue, not without justification, that this administration is unable to claim any major foreign policy success. Although such statements might generate partisan quibbling over the invasion of Grenada, it is clear that the Reagan administration's record in the Middle East represents a failure. In part this may be attributed to the often overlooked fact that the administration has had three different national security advisors as well as two secretaries of state. Relations among Reagan's top advisors have frequently been troubled and the administration has found it difficult to formulate a coherent, rational, and long-term policy. As a result, the United States during the Reagan presidency has had three different and at times conflicting policies towards the Middle East. These three phases

are readily identifiable and are discussed below.
Their antecedents are somewhat less clear, but seem to
have their origins in a complicated melange of bureaucratic infighting, problems in transforming ideological
electoral slogans into pragmatic and efficacious policies, the risks inherent in using military means to
resolve political problems, and the administration's
unwillingness or inability to forge strong, durable,
and clearly defined relations with U.S. supporters in
the region.

Phase One--Strategic Consensus

In terms of American influence in the Middle East,
the Carter administration bequeathed a not unenviable
legacy. The hostages had finally been released from
the embassy in Tehran, the Camp David accords still
seemed viable, and Soviet influence in the region was
diminishing. Yet while President Carter's term in office was heralded by an unprecedented and unrealistic
emphasis on human rights issues, Reagan's was characterized by his stated concern with Soviet expansionism
and international terror. At the time, this was viewed
as campaign rhetoric geared to providing Reagan with an
air of tough decisiveness which would contrast strongly
with popular views of Carter as indecisive and timid.
Yet Reagan the candidate and Reagan the president were
one and the same. Portraying sensitive and politically
significant Middle East issues within an East-West
framework, the President and Secretary of State Alexander Haig put a high priority on the maintenance of regional stability, which they perceived as a direct out-
growth of a concomitant and vigorous resistance to
Soviet force projections. The anticipated growth of
the Rapid Deployment Force and increased arms sales
throughout the region were meant, in large part, to
achieve such goals.
It is obvious that the Reagan administration
learned the appropriate lessons from the Soviet invasion of Afghanistan. Regrettably, however, an exaggerated emphasis on Soviet Middle East involvement overlooked other potentially destabilizing factors. For
example, the Iranian Revolution caused far greater
problems for the United States yet was not the product
of Soviet machinations. As a report issued by the Carnegie Endowment argued in 1981:

> Challenges to American interests in the Persian
> Gulf are more likely to be political...than mili-
> tary, and the military threats are more likely to
> come from within the region than from Moscow.[3]

As the Reagan presidency began, there was little evidence to suggest Soviet expansion in the Middle East, while the potentials for national and regional political unrest were as high as ever. Strangely, American Middle East policy found itself in the ill-advised position of ignoring the object of its stated concern-- the Middle East. Such key events as the Iran-Iraq War, the assassination of President Sadat, the Israeli bombings of Beirut and Baghdad, the takeover of the Grand Mosque in Saudi Arabia, and, perhaps most importantly, the Iranian Revolution, highlight the dangers of losing sight of the trees for the forest.

Strategic consensus was primarily an expansion and articulation of the Carter doctrine and the concept of the Rapid Deployment Force. Presupposing a fear of Soviet expansion among Middle Eastern leaders comparable in magnitude to its own, the Reagan foreign policy team sought to create an anti-Soviet entente. By binding the moderate Arab states, Israel, and the United States together in an undefined security arrangment, petty regional rivalries would be transcended as all stood shoulder to shoulder against the Soviets. This simple-minded notion was and remains flawed for several reasons. First, many Arab states fear Israel far more than they do the Soviets. This was certainly the message conveyed to Secretary of State Alexander Haig on a trip to Saudi Arabia in April 1981. Second, a particularly insidious form of Soviet-sponsored instability may take the form of support for indigenous opposition or terrorist groups. It is difficult to imagine American troops supporting Saudi troops for example, in the face of domestic insurgence of any sort whether Soviet-inspired or not. Third, the Iranian Revolution enhanced a reluctance among regional elites to be perceived as being too close to the U.S. Thus, excessively close ties with the U.S. might promote the very sorts of challenges to stability that they were created to oppose.

All of the above is not meant to argue that a Soviet threat does not exist. Rather, a more balanced policy is needed which is cognizant both of the nature of politics in the region and the manner in which the Soviets are involved in them. The Soviet Union did invade Afghanistan, its first major military movement beyond its own bloc since World War II. Furthermore, the Soviets are intimately involved in Syria, South Yemen, and Libya. It should not be forgotten, however, that they have supported both sides in the Iran-Iraq War, that they were expelled from Egypt after heavy involvement, that their influence in Iraq has deteriorated, and that the nature of their costly and prolonged involvement in Afghanistan is likely to make them reluctant to project power elsewhere in the region. In short, the Soviet position in the Middle East is

unenviable. To assume total Soviet control of clients
is fallacious. Recent events in Syria support argu-
ments that "the Syrian tail wags the Soviet dog."
Muammar Qaddaffi, not the Soviet Union, dominates
Libyan foreign policy.

Although strategic consensus was meant to bridge
gaps in the Middle East, for the most part it widened
them. Who can forget the controversy over the sale of
AWACs and F-15 equipment to the Saudis? And the com-
pensatory sale to Israel of additional F-15s hardly in-
spired Arab confidence in the United States.

In short, strategic consensus dominated half of
Reagan's presidency yet accomplished nothing. More importantly, it entailed the abandonment of Camp David by
the United States. With no incentive to seek West Bank
autonomy, the next phase of the process, Israel continued building settlements at a pace which culminated
in the de facto annexation of the occupied territories.
The primary victim of the abandonment was President
Sadat who justified the Camp David accords by promising
more rapid Egyptian economic development and progress
towards resolution of the Palestine problem. He failed
on both counts and his death was welcomed rather than
lamented in most corners of Egypt and the Arab world.
Having wasted its first two years in office, the Reagan
administration realized that it was high time to re-
enter the arena of Middle East policy.

Phase Two--The Reagan Initiative

The replacement of Alexander Haig by George Shultz
as secretary of state brought an immediate end to Washington's policy vacuum in the Middle East. Shultz
opted for pragmatism rather than ideology as he sought
ways to compensate for almost two years of American
inactivity. The result was President Reagan's speech
on the Middle East of September 1, 1982.

The Reagan speech was a remarkable departure from
the administration's stance during its first two years
in office. Recognizing that abandonment of Camp David
had been a costly blunder, the President compensated
unconvincingly by noting that: "...we never lost sight
of the next step of Camp David (i.e., West Bank autonomy talks)...it was not until January 1982 that we were
able to make a major effort to renew these talks."[4]
The most startling feature of the speech, however, lay
in Reagan's assertion that:

> The question now is how to reconcile Israel's le-
> gitimate security concerns with the legitimate
> rights of the Palestinians. And that answer can
> only come at the negotiating table. Each party
> must recognize that the outcome must be acceptable

to all and that true peace will require compromises by all.[5]

Statements such as these formed the core of the Reagan
initiative. The President went farther than any American president in history in publicly recognizing both
the existence of a Palestine problem and its centrality
to resolution of the Arab-Israeli conflict. Agreeing
that the "Palestinian...cause is more than a question
of refugees," the President shifted the focus of his
Middle East policy from confrontation with the Soviets
back to Camp David.[6] His unequivocally strong statement in favor of legitimate Palestinian rights was comparable to statements made by Presidents Ford and
Carter only after they had left office. Arguably, the
Reagan speech may be perceived as one of the most important American policy statements made about the Middle East in the past 30 years. Yet its uncharacteris-
tic balance, the apparent lack of advance coordination
with Middle Eastern leaders, and its significant swing
away from earlier policy directions doomed the initiative from the start. Recognition of the importance of
the Palestine issue, rare for any American president,
seemed particularly incongruous from one as conservative as Reagan. Furthermore, immediate rejection of
the initiative by Israel piqued Arab interest while
making its viability even more questionable.

The thrust of the initiative lay in its reliance
on Jordanian support. It was recognized that Israel is
unwilling to negotiate with the PLO under any circumstances. It might, however, deal with the Jordanians
while some sort of joint Israeli-Jordanian option for
West Bank autonomy seemed a realistic goal. The stick-
ing point lay in inducing participation by King Hussein. Another problem lay in Israeli rejection, which
was a blow to the President's prestige; dismissal of a
major foreign policy initiative by a close ally was
indeed embarrassing.

While the pace of West Bank settlement clearly
worried King Hussein, who saw the occupied territories
permanently disappearing from Arab control, he realized
the risks of "swimming upstream," e.g., the fate of
Anwar Sadat. The Jordanian monarch's caution is
matched only by his political longevity--a not unrea-
sonable trade-off given the fate of mavericks in the
Middle East. Given the history of Jordan, Hussein was
acutely aware of his vulnerability to the turbulent
vicissitudes of Palestinian politics. The way out of
this quagmire was through direct negotiation with Yas-
sir Arafat from whom a mandate for negotiation with
Israel was sought.

In the spring of 1983 intensive negotiations between Hussein and Arafat began. Thus, despite Israel's
outright rejection of the American scheme, the public

relations benefits of appearing more flexible than the Israelis played a role in PLO/Jordanian consideration of the Reagan plan. And by all accounts King Hussein was eager to become involved. Arafat, with his survivor's commitment to keeping all his Arab supporters happy, rejectionists and moderates alike, was more skeptical.

One by-product of Hussein's desire to pursue the Reagan plan was a severe split between Palestinians and Jordanians within Jordan.[7] This split has always existed but never was more evident than during the period of Arafat's visit to Amman. Palestinians in Jordan were at best ambivalent about Hussein's becoming involved, Jordanians were strongly opposed. It was felt that negotiations with Israel over the West Bank were hopeless, Israel had already annexed the territories in a de facto sense, and the King of the Jordanians would be wasting his limited prestige and jeopardizing his throne by throwing in his lot with the U.S., which was unpredictable and unrealistic.

There was some justification for this opposition. Israel had already rejected the plan, and historically Israel has not been terribly susceptible to American pressure. Indeed, the U.S. has always been reluctant to push Israel at all, even in a limited, short-term fashion. Israel's Likud governments had clearly committed themselves to retention of the West Bank. Israel's unwillingness to talk, combined with the fact that talks were likely to produce nothing, makes Hussein's fascination with the Reagan plan seem somewhat naive. The U.S. on the other hand, was strongly committed to Jordanian participation upon which the entire plan hinged. But the U.S. provided nothing which Hussein could bring to Arafat, or to his own people for that matter, to demonstrate American good faith. Had the U.S. pressed for a settlement freeze, even of the most limited sort, this might have facilitated Hussein's quest for a Palestinian mandate. The U.S. offered nothing but vague promises. Given America's lack of credibility throughout the Middle East, Hussein's eventual rejection of the Reagan initiative should not have come as a surprise.

Phase Three--Strategic Cooperation

Both strategic consensus and the Reagan initiative exhausted themselves quickly. The failure of the latter was particularly frustrating for the president, who expended a good deal of personal prestige and gained nothing. These issues were soon overshadowed, however, by America's costly and controversial involvement in Lebanon, which provided an important stimulus to phase three of its changing Middle East policy.

To the American public, U.S. forces in Lebanon were portrayed as nonpartisan peace-keepers. Their actual role was to prop up Amin Jumayyil whom some wryly called "the Mayor of Beirut." It rapidly became evident that American policies in Lebanon exacerbated an already difficult situation. What American policymakers had hoped was that through support for the Jumayyil central government and the Lebanese army, which the U.S. would train and arm, the necessary stability for negotiations among Lebanon's contending groups could be achieved. What was needed, however, was a genuinely neutral, U.N.-sponsored multinational force, rather than one which unconvincingly feigned impartiality. Both America and Israel supported Jumayyil publicly and with excessive fanfare. Such support emphasized Jumayyil's dependence on foreign interests rather than portraying him as the type of Lebanon-first patriot who might achieve some measure of success in search of national unity.

Given that the U.S. and Israel had shared views on what would be politically desirable for Lebanon, and the American perception that Lebanon was more serious than the West Bank, Washington was compelled to focus more attention on the former than on the latter where the Reagan initiative seemed doomed to failure.

It soon became clear that withdrawal of the marines from Beirut might well spell the end of the Jumayyil government. On the other hand, a continued American military presence presented the Reagan administration with unacceptably high political risks at home. Frustrated by Syria's reluctance to withdraw and by King Hussein's unwillingness to single-handedly endorse the Reagan initiative, Israel's strategic importance to the United States was enhanced.

The product of this realization was America's third Middle East policy in as many years--strategic cooperation. Having its origins in an earlier memo on cooperation signed by Caspar Weinberger and Ariel Sharon (later annulled by the U.S.), strategic cooperation was not a dramatic departure from traditional American policies in that it tended to formalize and codify the historically close ties between the U.S. and Israel. Such asymmetry has become characteristic of American-Middle Eastern relations, with Israel always being the largest aid recipient and closest partner in the region. Historically, America has sought dual Middle East policies, one for Israel and another for the Arab world.

One of the virtues of Camp David was its attempt to transcend this gap through a policy acceptable to Israel, as well as to some segment of the more moderate Arab leadership. Strategic consensus had the same goal, and although it was a failure it at least recognized the troublesome task of sustaining two

policies simultaneously. The Reagan initiative, at
least in theory, went even farther as it boldly sought
a means to bring moderate Arab elements in addition to
Egypt into the peace process. In conception, it reflected America's potential role in the Middle East at
its best. That it was unimplementable or, perhaps because America lacked the will to make it viable, its
failure was a great tragedy for all parties in the
Arab-Israeli conflict. The greatest flaw in strategic
cooperation was that it represented a betrayal of the
spirit behind such policies--it encouraged Arab-Israeli
isolation rather than negotiation. Despite its high
costs, however, it was politically easier to achieve
than more even-handed policies.

The trauma of American military involvement in Lebanon forced policy-makers to seek short-term gains
with little consideration for middle and long-term
costs; policy towards the region as a whole was subordinated to the issue of American involvement in Lebanon. After first having tried to minimize Israeli involvement in Lebanon, the United States went full
circle and sought to increase it, to lower the pressure
on its own forces. Although many of the details of the
strategic cooperation arrangement have not been made
public, the United States paid well for it. Aid to
Israel was increased while the Israelis were given more
flexibility in its use. Despite such benefits, the
agreement caused concern even in Israel where some felt
that Prime Minister Shamir had committed himself to a
dangerous and costly course of action. As Abba Eban
noted at the time:

> ...it is our duty to tell our [American] friends
> that Israel will absolutely decline to invest the
> lives of its sons in the expulsion of Syrian
> forces or in the fantasy of a stable, united Leba-
> non under a Christian Phalangist leadership which
> has manifestly failed to assert its authority or
> to become the focus of a Lebanese consensus.[8]

Although Eban's remarks were not necessarily representative of Israeli public opinion, they did highlight
American perceptions of strategic cooperation. Although the terms "proxy" or "mercenary" were avoided,
they clearly lurked close to the surface in Eban's remarks.

By coming down so strongly on the side of Israel,
America complicated its relations with even the most
moderate Arab states. Egypt, Saudi Arabia, and Jordan
were all critical of the policy shift although public
criticism was somewhat muted. For example, America was
quick to express its delight at the December 1983 meeting between Yasser Arafat and Husni Mubarak in Cairo
after Arafat's humiliating departure from Beirut.

American support for the meeting naturally outraged the
Israelis just as strategic cooperation troubled the
Egyptians. Yet rapprochement with Egypt might have encouraged the PLO to support King Hussein's desire to
enter the Reagan initiative. On the other hand, strategic cooperation continued. The joint U.S.-Israeli
politico-military team hammered out an agreement which
included American access to Israeli medical facilities
when necessary, the stockpiling of American medical
equipment in Israel, and so on.

As the presidential elections and the Democratic
convention approached, the administration became increasingly concerned about the domestic political costs
of maintaining American forces in Lebanon. Thus, the
desirability of a continued Israeli presence in Lebanon. In American electoral terms, the controversial
American military involvement in Lebanon was politically more significant than were the costs of deterio-
rating relations with the moderate Arabs. One set of
policy interests mortgaged another.

Conclusions

As its first term in office came to an end, the
Reagan administration found itself at a crossroads in
its Middle East policy. On the eve of its bid for re-
election, the Reagan team was confronted by an array of
Democratic challengers all of whom except for Jesse
Jackson outdid one another in expressing their undying
support for Israel. The administration's opposition to
Congressional efforts to move the American Embassy from
Tel Aviv to Jerusalem, as well as President Reagan's
plea at a United Jewish Appeal gathering for support
for arms sales to Jordan quickly brought the Middle
East policy "season" to a halt. The policy goals of
the administration and its electoral ambitions clashed.
The American election, as well as those in Israel and,
to a lesser extent, in Egypt, pushed American policy
formulation to the backburner. The situation in Lebanon continued to deteriorate as the multilateral talks
in Lausanne failed. New problems arose as civil war
seemed imminent in the Sudan and the Iran-Iraq war
spilled over into the Persian Gulf with the two pro-
tagonists sinking ships and threatening oil supplies to
the West and Japan.

Given the strong likelihood that President Reagan
will be reelected, a number of significant Middle East
issues will demand attention. Yet the form this will
take remains murky. Much depends on the Israeli elections. The second component of the Camp David accords,
the quest for West Bank autonomy, depends heavily on
who occupies office in Israel. Although there are indications that the Labor Alignment would be more

forthcoming on this issue, there are those that argue
that Israel has passed the point of no return in its
settlement policies on the West Bank.[9]   Be that as it
may, the one bright spot in American policymaking during this period was the Reagan initiative. Ironically,
American policymakers crafted an approach whose very
even-handedness doomed it to failure. Creative and
courageous statesmen are in increasingly short supply
in the Middle East, and the competing goals of the primary antagonists render a "good" policy almost as frustrating as no policy at all. Like Camp David, the
Reagan initiative is one with great promise whose primary problem may be that it cannot realistically be
implemented. Perhaps this will not be the case if the
Labor Alignment comes to power in Israel. Yet frustra-
tions and false starts should not paralyze the peace
process, and the Reagan plan should be viewed as a
positive first step. It has taken America forward in
its dealings with the Middle East and subsequent administrations would be ill-advised to retreat from it. It
is the obligation of any administration in Washington
to live up to both the letter and the spirit of Camp
David which, after all, was as much an American accomplishment as it was Israeli and Egyptian.

NOTES

For helpful comments, I would like to thank Zvi
Gitelman, George Grassmuck, Steven Heydemann, and Barry
Rubin. Naturally, the usual exemptions from respon-
sibility apply.

1. For example, Israel's Minister of Finance has
asked for a slower pace in the building of West Bank
settlements and a cut in the defense budget in order to
lower Israel's anticipated 400 percent inflation rate
for this fiscal year. These budgetary changes have
already led to significant political conflict within
the ruling coalition.
2. For an excellent critique of American Middle
East policy in the early period of the Reagan presidency, see I. William Zartman, "The Power of American
Purposes," The Middle East Journal Vol. 35, No. 2
(Spring 1981), pp. 163-177.
3. Staff of the Carnegie Panel on U.S. Security
and the Future of Arms Control, Challenges for U.S.
National Security; Assessing the Balance: Defense
Spending and Conventional Forces, Carnegie Endowment
for International Peace, 1981, p. 189.
4. Press Release of President Reagan's Speech on
the Middle East, September 1, 1982, p. 3.

5. Ibid., p. 5.

6. Ibid., p. 6.

7. Numerous interviews by the author in Amman with Palestinian and Jordanian academics, journalists, and policy makers in April 1983.

8. Abba Eban, "Bad Advice from Good Friends," The Jerusalem Post, 4 November 1983, p. 18.

9. The most authoritative work on this issue has been done by Israeli scholar/activist Meron Benvenisti. The West Bank Data Project: A Survey of Israel's Policies (Washington, D.C.: American Enterprise Institute, 1984) Studies in Foreign Policy.

3
The Government–Armed Forces Relationship

Zeev Schiff

The main difficulty in dealing with the sensitive
subject of the relationship between the government and
the armed forces in Israel lies in the danger of gener-
alizing. An additional danger stems from political
prejudices. Examples of this are stereotypical views
which hold that military personnel are extremist in
their viewpoints and, therefore, when they influence
the political echelon, it is always an extremist influence advocating the use of force.

It would also be a wrongful generalization to conclude that the army's influence reached a peak during
the Likud government headed by Begin.

In order to explain the relationship between the
military and the government while Begin was in power,
it is necessary to comment on the preceding period and
review the social structure of the Israeli Defense
Forces (IDF).

Whenever the political opinions of soldiers are
compared with those of civilians and politicians, the
general consensus is that military men adopt tougher
and more extreme positions. This holds true in almost
every place and society and is, not surprisingly, also
believed in Israel. Generals are usually expected to
be "square" and inflexible, with a strong inclination
to recommend the use of force, and a strong desire to
resolve conflicts by military means or--at the very
least--by the creation of the options afforded by
threats. In Israel, people of such mind used to be
accused of seeing the Israel-Arab problem through the
"sights of a rifle."

If is difficult to avoid generalizations when dis-
cussing the opinions of any group, yet--in making the
Israeli comparison--it seems that the political leadership is more extremist than the top brass of the Israel
Defense Forces or than the military community at large.
Anti-Arab slogans and the voicing of empty threats are
far more prevalent among politicians. This has always

been the case and is particularly so at the present
time.

Indeed, political moderation is one of the prime
characteristics of the present top echelon in the IDF;
it is certainly the attitude of the group that sets the
pace in the Israeli Command.

Of course, there are those who will argue that the
moderation of the top brass is a relatively new phenomenon, evident only since the Yom Kippur War and resulting from it. This war undoubtedly had a strong
influence, yet the tendency to moderation was prevalent
even beforehand. There is no better proof of the earlier existence of moderation in the higher ranks than
the leaders who have grown up in the IDF. Alongside
men like Ariel Sharon and Rafael Eitan--who can be defined as right-wing and as extremist in their views--
are many more senior officers who found their way into
the parties of the left or of moderation. Two prominent examples are Major-General Matityahu Peled and
Colonel Meir Pail, who can both be described as left-
wing and were active in the Sheli Party. More centrist
in their views are Major-General Aharon Yariv, past
head of intelligence, or Lieutenant-General Haim Bar
Lev, chief of staff of the IDF and his predecessor Yitzhak Rabin, and many others. All these men formed their
political opinions well before the Yom Kippur War, as
did Yigal Allon, a senior commander in the War of Independence.

This outline of prominent military personalities
proves clearly that the Israeli Army does not--nor can
it, because of its very nature--cultivate military
cliques. There have never been any signs of a junta
seeking to protect the army's own interests. For IDF
officers, at least for most of them, service in the
army is the ultimate expression of their desire to
serve the nation on one of its more critical fronts.
The only other common denominator is professional and
technical, certainly not political or factional.

The standing army is mostly composed of draft-
ees--aged 18-21--and partly of regulars. Reservists
are integrated at all levels of command and at all
times. Even among the regular army there are a great
many men who have stayed on only for a few years--and
not as a lifetime career. This is particularly true of
junior officers. Thousands of youngsters decide to
devote a few extra years to the security of the state
in addition to their compulsory service, yet resolve in
advance to return to civilian life. There is an essentially parallel process, though based on permanent procedures, among the higher ranks of the IDF Command.
All men who reach the rank of major-general know that
they have at most five more years of service in the
army. A major-general usually rotates through no more
than two postings at this rank. Few remain for a third

posting, and these men are generally considered to be
candidates for chief of staff. The turnover among general officers is high, with the result that a decisive
majority of IDF officers become civilians before their
fiftieth birthday. Most begin their second, civilian,
career somewhere between the ages of 45 and 48. This
not only prevents the crystallization of cliques, but
also necessarily compels IDF officers to operate with
their faces turned to the civil structure that must
absorb them at a younger age than in many other countries.

The Six-Day War and its results stimulated an involvement of military men in political life. Differences of opinion developed in the waiting period that
preceded the war. They had their beginnings in the
dispute and disagreement between the prime minister and
most of his colleagues on the one hand, and the majority of the general staff on the other, over intelligence
appraisals and the view that the political echelon had
trailed behind them hesitantly. The commanders became
national heroes. They departed from their relative
anonymity to a new place in the limelight of greatly
exaggerated publicity.

After the Six-Day War, many IDF commanders permitted themselves, from a political standpoint, to do
things never previously considered. They began to intervene, directly and indirectly, in matters of political significance--this was true of both the moderates
and the extremists. Their interests covered the spectrum from borders, settlement in the territories, to
questions of reaction to Soviet involvement in the Middle East and negotiation with the United States for
settlement with Israel's neighbors.

The political leadership facilitated this development. Parties chased after the soldiers. Since they
were national heroes, they were welcome additions to
the ranks of political organizations. In this fashion
Major-General Ezer Weizman moved directly from the general staff to the cabinet as minister of transport, and
Lieutenant-General Haim Bar Lev stepped straight from
the chief of staff's office to that of the minister of
commerce and industry. Frequently the parties nego-
tiated with officers while they were still in uniform.
Major-General Sharon came straight out of the IDF to
start organizing the right-wing parties into one bloc,
the Likud. Major-General Aharon Yariv also took a
short route from the army to a political position, and
soon to a post as minister in the government.

The astounding thing is that, of all people, Moshe
Dayan--Ben-Gurion's student and disciple--accepted it
calmly. Not only didn't he fight against it, but he
indirectly contributed to its development. By contrast
with Ben-Gurion, Defense Minister Dayan agreed that the
chief of staff should become a permanent fixture at

cabinet meetings. Perhaps Dayan wanted to relieve himself of the responsibility for certain critical security matters--or at least share it with his subordinates.
Once the fence was broken, and the chief of staff became a regular participant, it was impossible to deny
the privilege to other officers--and so they were in-
vited, from time to time, to express their opinions to
the cabinet. This was the situation when the Likud
rose to power.

When exploring the relationship between the military and the government during Begin's time, it becomes
clear that there is a significant difference between
the first and second cabinets. These differences are
very sharp. In retrospect, it appears that the person
who has had the most influence on the course of events
is the minister of defense--more so than the entire
government.

The first minister of defense in Begin's first
government was Ezer Weizman who was considered a war-
monger as an army man, but a moderate as a political
leader. Weizman's first decision as defense minister
was to implement a significant cut in the defense
budget. This was an extraordinary move. It was contrary to the military's position and against the recommendation of the minister of defense who preceded him,
Shimon Peres. Peres urged Weizman to increase the
budget because, according to his assessment, war with
Syria was not far off.

The most important incident in the relationship
between the military and the government, while Weizman
was minister of defense, happened later on, after
Sadat's visit to Jerusalem. The issue was whether to
agree to Sadat's demands to give back the entire Sinai
Peninsula in return for peace. The general staff of
the IDF prepared a plan in which only part of the Sinai
would be returned to Egypt in the first phase. The
recommendation of the general staff spoke of a division
of the Sinai. It insisted that two vital areas of the
Sinai should stay in Israel's hands, even after the
peace accord.

The general staff was surprised because Begin and
Dayan had essentially already promised the entire Sinai
to Sadat, before consulting with the military leaders.
In fact, no discussions at all were held on the general
staff's proposal. No consideration was given to their
recommendation. This happened during Begin's first
government. In all probability, something like this
never would have happened with Eshkol, Golda Meir or
Yitzhak Rabin. A decision of great significance to
national security would never have been made by a Labor
government without first consulting with the general
staff.

Begin's first government was totally different
in composition from his second. His first cabinet

consisted of persons with military backgrounds including two former chiefs of staff--Yigal Yadin and Moshe Dayan; and a defense minister, Ezer Weizman, who was deputy chief of staff and chief of the Air Force. During the first period when Begin assumed the position of defense minister, Zipori, who had military experience, was deputy minister. Later, he was pushed out of his position and was not put on the minister's committee for defense affairs.

One of the main reasons for the insufficient civilian control over the armed forces since 1980 derives from the fact that Begin's second cabinet has lacked real experience in defense matters. Despite the average young age of its ministers, most of them did not serve in the IDF, which is a very unusual phenomenon in Israel.

The changes began when Begin was acting as minister of defense. It was a period of loss of control--of ineffective civilian supervision of the defense establishment. As a result, the chief of staff actually became the minister of defense. Begin's admiration for uniforms and for everything connected to the Israeli military permitted this development to occur. The fact that Chief of Staff Raphael Eitan possessed extreme hawkish views set the course.

The actual turning point in the relationship between government and military occurred when Sharon was appointed minister of defense. All the rules of the game changed. Sharon's views and methods, which were expressed in the war in 1982, are better understood today.

This war produced a politico-military phenomenon without precedent in the history of Israel. Israel is a thoroughly democratic country, but on the eve of the war and in its initial phases something occurred which can only be described as a putsch--a novel kind of putsch, in which the army and its operations were commandeered to flout governmental decisions in matters of crucial importance. It was not the army that engineered the sophisticated putsch, but the man in charge of the army on behalf of the government, on behalf of the civil establishment, the defense minister. Sharon acted contrary to the government's intentions and sent the IDF into action to do things and serve purposes for which there was no governmental decision and of which the cabinet was kept in ignorance. Sharon implemented his very own plans, on which his mind was set long before the outbreak of the war. The IDF was his stooge, his instrument.

The result was that the cabinet did not know what was going on in the general staff, or received information too late. Sharon separated the ministers from the armed forces and isolated the cabinet.

Sharon manipulated the government through the medium of the IDF. He did not do this in the manner of regular putsch, as commonly practiced in the Middle East. The IDF was not sent in to take over the country's democratic institutions. Sharon did not seize the state television and radio stations. He did not shut down the Knesset and he did not arrest or dismiss ministers, nor did he clamp down on the Israeli press. His method was more sophisticated--a covert putsch. Here was an Israeli innovation, whereby the army acted against the will and the intentions of the government, but without its changing the democratic structure of the country. The democratic framework stayed in place, but in the process its ability to act was undermined. Here is a method that can certainly provide political scientists with plenty of food for thought.

Some senior IDF officers sensed what was going on and suspected that the government was being maneuvered. Certain officers made critical remarks at meetings of the general staff and raised questions whether this or that move had been approved by the government and whether operations in the field were not opposed to cabinet resolutions. But on the whole the IDF high command reaction was overly passive. Given to discipline as a matter of course, they overdid it on this occasion. This led to a moral crisis when, subsequently, the full picture came to light.

The departure of Sharon from the defense ministry brought certain changes. Sharon's era in the defense ministry came to its end before the cabinet had approved the report of the Kahan Commission--established to investigate the extent of Israeli involvement in the events in Sabra and Shatila in September 1982--which recommended that Sharon be replaced due to his responsibility, and before his official resignation. Sharon tried to mobilize the general staff on his side, to put pressure on the cabinet in order to challenge the Kahan report. He wanted to create the impression in the cabinet that if they voted for his resignation they would harm the armed forces. The general staff turned its back on him. The chief of staff, General Eitan, published an Order of the Day which he read personally in public, saying that the IDF accepts the Kahan report as a court decision. This move was a symbolic divorce of the IDF from Sharon.

The new defense minister, Moshe Arens, has tried to calm the IDF and to listen more carefully to their voices. Although he supported the idea of war against the PLO in Lebanon, Arens understood that he had to change the initial war objectives. Without many public declarations he turned them from the offensive to the defensive approach. He has adopted a more realistic line; the defense of the Galilee and not of Amin Jumayyil's government in Beirut. He supported the

withdrawal of the IDF from the Shuf region. After the
abrogation of the May 17 Israeli-Lebanese agreement,
however, Arens opposed an additional withdrawal, because of military reasons, and probably also because of
the upcoming elections.

In sum, it is clear that Sharon's period harmed
the armed forces and damaged military morale. After
his forced departure from the defense ministry, there
existed strong suspicion and alienation between many of
the officers and the politicians. Prime Minister
Shamir, who replaced Menachem Begin, is still connected
to the war in Lebanon, and it is doubtful if he and his
cabinet will make the necessary structural and institu-
tional changes to improve civilian control of the armed
forces. If the Labor party is elected on July 23,
there is a chance that the new prime minister will
establish a staff organization, roughly equivalent to
the American National Security Council, which will provide the prime minister, the cabinet, and especially
the Ministerial Committee on Security Affairs, with
policy papers. This might, indirectly, provide the
cabinet with a better flow of information.

4
Israel After Begin: The View From the Religious Parties

Gary S. Schiff

It is somewhat ironic that the religious political parties of Israel, which were first "discovered" by the outside world at the time Menachem Begin and his Likud party came to power in 1977, have now, with the departure of Begin from the political scene, been dismissed as unimportant. Both their "discovery" and their dismissal are, to paraphrase Mark Twain, grossly exaggerated and premature.

The religious political parties are an integral part of Israel's political fabric. They are "independent variables" of any other political party or leader. Barring major alterations to the political system and social composition of the country, the religious political parties are likely to remain a potent political force for many years to come. Despite recent reverses in the political fortunes of these parties, in the near to mid-term their influence is likely to increase rather than to decline in the post-Begin era.

What are the Religious Parties?

While this is not the proper place to engage in a detailed historical analysis of the development of these political parties, a capsulized description of their distinguishing characteristics is in order.[1] First, it is important to note that the religious political parties of Israel, unlike those of Western Europe, claim to represent the same religion, indeed the same denomination of that religion, i.e., the Orthodox variant of Judaism. It is perhaps for this reason that they are often lumped together indiscriminately by outside observers as having common characteristics and similar political behaviors. Such terms as "conservative," "clericalist," "right wing," etc., are often used in this connection.

In fact, the religious parties are very different and have clearly distinguishable political and social characteristics, as well as often divergent roles within the Israeli political system. Initially each of these parties developed as different reactions to the modernization of Jewish life in Europe in the 19th century, and particularly to the challenge of modern political secular Jewish nationalism or Zionism.

The largest of these political parties, the National Religious Party (NRP), or in its Hebrew acronym Mafdal, is as its name implies a religious nationalist party. It is essentially positively oriented towards modernity, seeking an accommodation between religious belief and behaviors, on the one hand, and the exigencies of modern life, on the other. Thus, it has long had a participatory attitude towards the Zionist movement and the State of Israel, which it views as both a political framework and as a genuinely religious phenomenon, a prophecy come true.

Thus, its perennial participation in the political system--Mafdal has historically been the essential junior coalition partner to the dominant political party, whether Labor or Likud--has been accompanied by a largely successful attempt at institutionalizing religion within the overall political and legal framework of the state. Mafdal is, therefore, the dominant force in the official religious establishment of the state. It is, nevertheless, a party run by lay leadership, with a broad socioeconomic, geographic and ethnic base.

The other principal religious party, Agudat Yisrael, developed out of the opposite or negative reaction of traditional European Jewry to the challenges of modernity, secularism and the Zionist movement. The result was a separatist and/or autonomist mentality opposed to the inroads of modernism and secularism into the traditional Jewish community. As such, the party was originally anti-Zionist. Since the Holocaust and the rise of the State of Israel, however, it has taken an instrumentalist view of the State of Israel, accepting it as a de facto secular political authority to be dealt with like other government authorities, but not, as in the case of the Mafdal, as a religious phenomenon to be cherished in its own right.

Agudat Yisrael is essentially clerically dominated, with a limited socioeconomic, geographic and ethnic constituency, confined largely to certain cities and neighborhoods and subethnic groups (overwhelmingly Eastern European). The party--sometimes with its break-away labor wing, Poalei Agudat Yisrael (PAY), sometimes without it--has participated in government coalitions from time to time, but more frequently has not. Whereas Mafdal has been the backbone of government coalitions of both the Labor and the Likud governments, Agudat Yisrael has participated only very selectively. Its current somewhat anomalous position, as a participant in the coalition but not as an integral part of the cabinet itself, is characteristic of its tentative and pragmatic approach to dealing with Israeli governments. As opposed to Mafdal, whose interests are broad, Agudah's scope of involvement is largely limited to the protection and provision of services to its constituency, whether religious, educational or social.

The divergent fundamental ideological natures of these religious political parties are reflected in their different internal political structures, in the social composition of their votership and their leadership, and in their very different forms of political behavior within the system. While they are altogether a relatively small minority within the system, never garnering more than approximately 15 percent of the total vote (roughly 10% for Mafdal, 5% for the Agudah parties), they have wielded political power far in excess of their numbers. This is in large part due to their critical make-or-break position in terms of Israel's multiparty coalition government system which, thanks to the state's very pure proportional representation voting system, magnifies the power of relatively small political parties.

Too often overlooked, however, is the fact that these parties do represent an important source of residual legitimacy for the state. For many in the general public, both in Israel and in Jewish communities abroad, they embody much of what is perceived as the traditional Jewish ethos. And while the salience of this ethos and all that it represents is not sufficient to have ever appreciably increased the percentages of voting for these parties, there is nevertheless a lingering affinity towards them by many in the general public. This holds true except when they press religious issues beyond the point of public acceptance, whether these issues deal with public transportation on the Sabbath, archeological digs, autopsies, military service for women, or the knotty question of "Who is a Jew?"

Recent Political Trends:
Factionalism and Ethnicity

Just as 1977 had been viewed as a banner year for the religious parties, with Mafdal garnering twelve seats in the 120-seat Knesset and Agudat Yisrael five, for a total of seventeen, the Knesset elections of 1981 were widely viewed as a disaster. The political strength of Mafdal was cut in half from twelve to six seats. Even the less volatile Agudat Yisrael declined by one seat to four.

This downturn is largely attributable, at least insofar as Mafdal is concerned, to the fact that

several breakaway splinter parties, based largely on
ethnic criteria, had emerged. Some of Mafdal's Sephardi voters--who are now the majority in Mafdal--were
attracted to newly established personalistic factions
headed by leaders of their own subethnic groups. If
one adds the votes syphoned off by these groups, the
political balance is essentially restored. The fact
that ethnic parties have never succeeded in Israel,
while often tried in the past, affords some measure of
assurance that the historic pattern will reassert itself, though as indicated below, there are some signs
that this time things might be qualitatively different.
In more recent months the internal factional squabbling
within Mafdal has resulted in one of its six remaining
Knesset members withdrawing from the party's delegation
in the Knesset and forming his own parliamentary faction. This infighting has also led to some intense and
highly publicized conflict between the principal leaders of the party, based in its two main factions.
These events have led some observers to conclude that
the decline of the NRP is permanent and its disintegra-
tion into still smaller personalistic factions is imminent and inevitable. Rather, these developments represent a pattern of behavior that is characteristic of
Israeli parties in general, and of the religious
parties in particular, and not a fundamental dissolu-
tion of the component parts of the party. This intense
factionalism can be explained to a lesser extent in
ideological and historical terms, and to a greater degree by personal and especially generational conflicts,
the likes of which have been seen many times in Mafdal's past. Nevertheless, the party has historically
exhibited a remarkable resiliency and an ability to
recoup and rally around issues fundamental to it, such
as its basic commitment to religion and Zionism.

The Religious Parties and Likud

     With the rise of Menachem Begin to power in 1977,
his formation of a coalition with Mafdal (and to a
lesser extent Agudat Yisrael) was a timely, natural and
almost inevitable--if anything in politics is ever in-
evitable--development in the life of the religious parties, especially Mafdal. Since 1967, and especially
since 1973, Mafdal had come to emphasize its national-
istic credentials above even its religious ones, and
certainly over its vestigial socialist identity, which
remained strong only among its kibbutzim, old-time
labor union types and some ideologues. Thus, despite
the fact that Labor and Mafdal had long had a "historic
partnership," the ideological, let alone the electoral
bases for the partnership had been seriously eroded.

The partnership with Begin and the Likud, on the other hand, promised to be significantly more rewarding for a variety of reasons. On nationalist grounds, Begin clearly had superior credentials to his Labor counterparts. As the importance of the nationalist component had risen markedly for Mafdal--after all, its own young people were well represented among those who were joining Gush Emunim and setting up settlements on the West Bank--the Likud connection promised a clearer and more immediate fulfillment of long deferred but recently reawakened ideological goals.

On the ethnic front, the strong support of Begin and the Likud among Sephardi voters dovetailed with Mafdal's own somewhat belated attempt to give greater representation and visibility to its own Sephardi con- stituency, which by now was a clear majority of its voters.

On socioeconomic grounds, while there were still remnants of the old socialist Ha-Po'el Ha-Mizrachi labor movement ideologues around in the kibbutzim and elsewhere in the party, the emerging younger leadership was clearly urban, professional and middle class. It was not troubled by Likud's "bourgeois" ideology and free market economics, nor by jettisoning the shopworn slogans of socialist egalitarianism that had long since been abandoned in practice by much of the Labor party itself. Even on purely religious issues, while the bulk of the Likud party itself was essentially as secu- lar in orientation as Labor, the much vaunted personal traditionalism of Begin appeared to augur well for the realization of Mafdal's historic agenda.

For Agudat Yisrael, it was precisely Begin's re- spect for tradition which made him an ideal partner. Not particularly interested in foreign policy or in military matters, and having no particular vested in- terest in settlements, whether in Israel, the West Bank or elsewhere, Agudah found Begin a most amenable and cooperative partner in securing such services and meet- ing such demands as its limited constituency was wont to make.

The Religious Parties under Begin

In assessing the Begin era's impact on the reli- gious parties, it is clear that the more narrowly de- fined, specifically religious needs of Agudat Yisrael were more easily satisfied than the more complex con- cerns of Mafdal. Thus, the banning of flights on Saturdays by the national airline, El Al, or the liber- alization of the policy of exemption of religious women from military service, or the increased allocations to religious institutions--all provided for in coalition agreements--sufficed to satisfy the basic demands of

Agudat Yisrael. Nevertheless, the recurrent demand for
an amendment to the Law of Return specifying that only
conversions "according to halakhah (Jewish religious
law)" are recognized for purposes of immigration and
citizenship was not fulfilled.

At the same time the expectations of the broader
Mafdal constituency were not as readily or uniformly
met. Whereas Begin's first political act as prime
minister in 1977 was to visit the West Bank settlement
of Elon Moreh (Kaddum), the greatest achievement of his
first--if not of his entire--administration was the
conclusion of the historic peace treaty with Egypt.
While laudable in itself, the agreement did necessitate
the staged withdrawal from the Sinai, including the
town of Yamit, which Begin had vowed to retain. The
sharp division of opinion in Mafdal between its hawks
and doves over the treaty with Egypt not only precipitated some of the renewed ideologically-based factionalism, but also raised grave doubts in the minds of the
ascendent nationalist forces in Mafdal as to the depth
of Begin's commitment to the maximalist nationalist
cause. These parties continue to prefer Likud's overall orientation on these issues to that of Labor.

Likewise, the explosion of the Sephardi ethnic
factor in the course of the initial Begin victory may
be viewed as having engendered at least some of the
serious ethnic vote losses of Mafdal in the 1981 elections, as Sephardi voters gravitated to newly founded
Sephardi electoral lists. Yet, again, these ethnic
splinter parties have in the past been transitory
rather than permanent features of Israeli political
life. Nevertheless, there are indications that this
time things may be different and that the Sephardim are
learning to institutionalize their interests into permanent political groupings. Thus, for example, the
Tami party, led by former Mafdal minister Aharon Abu-
hatzeira, has formed the appropriate nonprofit corporations necessary to obtain government funding for its
educational and religious institutions. Similarly, a
Sephardi list of Agudat Yisrael ran successfully in the
Jerusalem municipal elections.

On the socioeconomic front, the liberalization of
the economy has not ended Israel's chronic economic
problems--inflation, imbalance of payments, low productivity. And on religious issues, much of the initiative has been preempted by Agudat Yisrael, responding
to the increasingly rightist tendencies of the Orthodox
community worldwide. This phenomenon, which has its
analogs in the rise of fundamentalist Islam and Chris-
tianity, is characterized by intensified personal pie-
tism and ritualism, as well as by increased intolerance
towards non-Orthodox Jews. Yet, Mafdal did break important new ground in its attempt to broaden the scope
of its issues and involvement. It finally achieved the

long-coveted post of minister of education, and perhaps
more significantly, that of deputy foreign minister,
signaling its emergence into a truly nationalist, even
internationalist party rather than a purely domestic
religious body.

The Religious Parties in the Post-Begin Era

And what of the future, the post-Begin era? How
will the religious parties fare? In the short term,
the replacement of Begin by the far less traditional
Shamir would not seem to augur well for the Agudat Yisrael, which seeks an essentially religious accommodation in the more narrowly defined sense. Thus, Shamir
can more easily renege, for example, on the personal
promise given by Begin to Agudat Yisrael in the last
coalition agreement that the Law of Return would be
amended to include the words "conversion according to
halakhah." This lack of personal commitment by Shamir
to traditional values may be the single greatest obsta-
cle to Agudat Yisrael's further political victories.
After all, its most successful political tool is the
historic "shtadlanut" (special appeals) approach to
government, whereby community representatives appear
before powerful government officials to plead the case
of the Jewish people--or, in this case, of the Orthodox
community.
At the same time, Agudat Yisrael is still an important piece in the present coalition puzzle. Agudat
Yisrael itself is under pressure from the ever more
right-leaning Orthodox community for even greater
achievements on the religious front, and therefore, is
likely to press these issues with single-minded determination. Therefore, Shamir is not likely to alienate
Agudah over issues which he may consider less than
central, but which they regard as high priority. Thus,
while personally less disposed towards religious demands, Shamir may indeed find it politic to at least
maintain the status quo.
The immediate future for Mafdal is less clear-cut.
The party is currently wracked by bitter internecine
factional conflict. As alluded to above, this conflict
is, on one level, largely a generational one, reflecting a long overdue change of guard between the present
leadership of the party, headed by 75-year-old Minister
of Interior Dr. Yosef Burg, who heads the Lamifneh faction, and the Tze'irim, the younger faction and its
leadership, centered around Minister of Education
Zevulun Hammer, and former Deputy Minister of Foreign
Affairs Dr. Yehudah Ben-Meir. Viewed from this
perspective, the factional conflict is a classic suc-
cession battle not unknown in other Israeli parties in
recent times.

However, the factional conflicts also have their strong ideological overtones. The old guard is more closely associated with the "historic partnership" with the Labor party, as well as with the vestiges of the old socialist, labor, agriculturally oriented, Ha-Po'el Ha-Mizrachi ideology. They are concerned with the more narrowly defined traditional issues on Mafdal's agenda, i.e., religion and education, and less with the broader political, military and economic concerns of the state. The old leadership is less militant in style, older and predominantly European-born.

The Tze'irim, on the other hand, are composed of younger native-born Sabras, who are products of the state religious school system long presided over by Mafdal. They are more intensely nationalist, and therefore closer to Likud in ideology. Similarly, they are more middle class, urban and career-oriented than their predecessors. Among them are some more Sephardim as well, again militating for a close tie to Likud. The style they prefer is more assertive and direct, more reminiscent of Begin than of the Labor leadership. Finally, having served in the military, they are concerned with military affairs, as well as with foreign policy and economic development and other more broadly defined issues.

Indeed, it is precisely this confluence of issues and ideology, as well as ethnic and generational ties, which precipitated the coalition between Likud and Mafdal beginning in 1977, and which will likely provide for its continuity under the Shamir administration even in the absence of Begin's personal charisma. Thus, the ascendance of the younger generation of Mafdal leaders is likely to strengthen ties with Likud, rather than weaken them.

Out of this factional squabbling will invariably emerge a new party leader and heir to Dr. Burg, which will in turn likely result in a concerted effort at the reunification and approximate restoration of its traditional strength, between ten and twelve Knesset seats, assuming that the effect of ethnic splinter parties will have played itself out. This move toward reconciliation will be true especially if there is a perceived threat of any kind, such as a Labor comeback and the possible political retribution that might engender such as taking away some of the cabinet posts won by Mafdal under the Likud. This is not to say, however, that if Labor should return to power Mafdal would not be sufficiently flexible to join a Labor-led coalition, and that Labor would not need and welcome Mafdal.

Indeed, with a strengthened and revitalized younger leadership the National Religious Party, despite its recent numerical decline and other setbacks, will likely become even more powerful and important in the intermediate range than hitherto. The quality of this leadership, and the scope of issues which it has targeted for itself is likely to render the party more assertive as well as more effective.

The rightist trend in Orthodoxy, mentioned above in connection with Agudat Yisrael, also affects Mafdal. In order to avoid preemption of religious issues by Agudat Yisrael, it is likely that Mafdal will also press religious concerns in an even more aggressive manner than in the past.

On its left flank, the expansion and renewed vigor of the non-Orthodox religious Jewish community in Israel, i.e., the Conservative and Reform movements, as they press for equal status and treatment, will more directly affect Mafdal than Agudah because of the murkier line of religious traditionalism between Conservative Jews and the modern Orthodox ones which Mafdal claims to represent. This, too, might precipitate a more right-wing stance on religious issues on the part of Mafdal, if only to distinguish itself from the newcomers. Other questions of considerable import to Mafdal are likely to be raised in the coming post-Begin years, particularly the question of the territories, especially the West Bank, in relation to the religious political parties, whether one considers this a domestic or foreign policy issue. The piece of real estate called the West Bank, more than any other of the territories (such as Gaza or Golan), raises fundamental ideological and policy questions for Mafdal.

Whereas Mafdal is often characterized as the "moderate" religious party on certain issues, the question of Judea and Samaria is seen not only as a political and security question, but also as a primary religious phenomenon, a fulfillment of prophecy, a justification of faith. This is not so for the so-called "extreme" religious party, Agudat Yisrael, which does not view the state of Israel as a religious manifestation and which therefore is much more flexible and pragmatic on this question.

For Mafdal, however, the settlement of the land does become a religious obligation. Conversely, the return of the land to Arab non-Jews is a gross violation of religious law. It is the graduates of Mafdal's educational system, not Agudah's, who have established settlements on the West Bank. And as mentioned above, it is the nationalist pillar of Mafdal ideology which has become the most important of its operational principles. Similarly, given the party's increasing concern with military and security issues, the West Bank has taken on an important strategic value as well. Likewise, the foreign policy implications of the West Bank question are now of great concern to Mafdal, and are likely to continue to bring it into closer orbit with Shamir and his Likud party than with Labor.

50

Apart from developments within the religious parties themselves, there are a number of systemic reasons
for believing that in the intermediate range the religious parties will maintain, if not strengthen their
roles within the system. As the 1981 elections demonstrated, Israel is moving away from a pure multiparty
system to what is essentially a two-and-one-half party
system, with Labor and Likud occupying the left-center
and right-center respectively, leaving only a small
area in the middle of the spectrum for another functioning political option. That option has traditionally been the religious one. Ironically, as the two
major parties grow stronger, larger, and closer to each
other in size, the religious parties, whether singly or
in concert, grow in proportional strength even as their
size shrinks. There are simply no alternatives to them
in the formation of a coalition. Thus, even if the
parties were not to recapture their high levels of
political support as in 1977, they would maintain their
key role within the political system.

Raising systemic issues, in turn, engenders considerations of a more long-term nature concerning the
viability of the religious political parties. In the
past there have been many attempts to alter Israel's
proportional representation system, which allows Knesset representation to any party receiving a mere one
percent of the vote, and thereby magnifies the power of
the smaller parties. All previous attempts at modifying this system somewhat--let alone jettisoning it in
the favor of a majority vote system--have failed,
largely due to the adamant and active opposition of the
many smaller parties. It is not inconceivable, however, for the two major parties at this point to re-
suscitate these proposals for a change in the electoral
system which, given the existing two-and-one-half party
nature of the system, might, in its extreme form, bring
about a genuine two-party system in the British mold.
Depending on the exact nature of such electoral reform,
the religious parties might decide to revert to a previous format, that of a United Religious Front, ideological differences notwithstanding. Such a move would
not necessarily guarantee their survival as separate
entities. Alternatively, as has been suggested, they
in fact might become specialized interest groups or
large factions within the two existing major parties.

However, as currently constituted, the electoral
system will provide for the continuation of the religious parties in their present form and for their continued centrality within the coalitional cabinet
system.

Other long-term factors affect religious parties
as well, and render their long-term future less secure.
One such factor is demography. While the birth rate
among Agudat Yisrael families tends to be considerably

above average in Israel, that of the more modernized
Mafdal adherents is only slightly so. The combined effect of this demographic phenomenon has resulted in a
steady decline in the percentage of Israeli school
children attending either the state religious (Mafdal-
dominated) or the independent (Agudat Yisrael-
controlled) school systems. From a high of over one-
third of the school population, the figure hovers not
much above one-quarter. As such, the smaller the proportion of the total population that is educated and
socialized in the school systems, and therefore the
values of the religious parties, the fewer voters they
will ultimately have. Of course, Agudat Yisrael has
the advantage of its cultural insularity and its fundamentalist ideology, which will assure continued adher-
ence to its tenets by its followers. However, this
phenomenon may well confine itself to a smaller and
smaller faction within the overall state and society.
    Mafdal, on the other hand, with its broader open-
ing to modern society, has always run the risk of losing its adherents to other political parties and movements. Given the fact that the party now consists of a
majority of Sephardim, many of these people may ultimately prefer to vote the Likud option--along with
maintaining a residual traditionalism in their life
styles--or to vote for an explicitly Sephardi party
altogether, rather than voting for a religious party
which happens to be nationalist as well. Assuming the
maintenance of the present electoral system, the long-
term viability of Mafdal, then, lies in its ability to
broaden the base of its constituencies and the scope of
its issues sufficiently for it to become a full-blown
national party without alienating its core group of
religious supporters. This is a difficult tightrope to
walk. In the long run, Mafdal will survive insofar as
it succeeds in becoming the Israeli equivalent of a
European Christian Democratic party, i.e., a centrist
party drawing its inspiration and values neither from
the socialist left nor the secular middle class right,
but rather from an updated and genuine Jewish political
and cultural tradition.
    This transformation will, in turn, engender a
fundamental and long deferred reexamination of the
"status quo" of religion and state questions, which has
prevailed in Israel since statehood and which the religious parties have defended and sought to extend. The
outcome of that reassessment, in which the religious
parties will inevitably have a major role and stake,
will have a profound impact not only on them but on the
future of the Israeli polity and democracy.

NOTES

1. Gary S. Schiff, <u>Tradition and Politics and the Religious Parties of Israel</u> (Detroit: Wayne State University Press, 1977).

5
Political Polarization: Contradictory Interpretations of Israeli Reality

Myron J. Aronoff

> The world grew bitter because the world fell
> somehow short of half-remembered Eden.[1]

One of the most striking developments in Israel in recent years is the reemergence of political polarization after nearly two decades of relative quietude. This polarization, which differs in several important respects from the divisiveness of the earlier period (to be discussed below), has been expressed largely through verbal violence, but there have also been dangerous signs of increasing physical violence as well. It is the result of the political coming of age and rise to power of formerly marginal groups which successfully challenged Labor's ideological and political dominance, and of the failure of Labor to adjust to its new status and to play a more constructive role in the opposition.

The Likud (the dominant political alignment in the coalition government since 1977) has attempted to establish its own dominance through the cooptation of new forms of religious nationalism and the exploitation of ethnic tensions. Labor, and a significant proportion of the members of kibbutzim, intellectuals, and others never fully accepted the legitimacy of the new government. Although they accepted the legality of the election results, they failed to accept the right of the Likud to impose its ideology and to implement policies which they argued lacked a national consensus. For the first time the two major political blocs, Labor and the Likud, with their conflicting perceptions and interpretations of reality, have equal political strength. Although the policies of the two major blocs have converged in several areas when compared with the earlier era, the leaders of each imply in their public positions that only their policies--particularly those pertaining to the future status of the territories

occupied by Israel in 1967 and the million Palestinians
residing within them--will ensure Israel's security,
and that their rival's are a threat to the nation's
survival. These conditions have resulted in the polarization of politics in Israel today.

 This essay analyzes the key incidents which led
to: (1) the intensification of the conflict between
the two camps in the periods prior to and after the
establishment of the state; (2) the 'normalization' of
relations in the later period; and (3) the renewal of
serious political strife in the contemporary period.

Early Polarization

 The early years of the developing Israeli society
and polity were characterized by relatively intense
ideological division and political competition particularly between the main political camps. This rivalry
was especially bitter between the Labor camp led by
David Ben-Gurion and the Revisionist movement led by
Vladimir Zeev Jabotinsky. After Jabotinsky's death he
was succeeded by his devoted disciple, Menachem Begin,
who carried on the struggle against Labor.

 The intensity of this ideological debate can be
attributed to a number of factors. Among the more important are the influence of Jewish tradition and culture, the intellectual and political climate of Eastern
Europe at the turn of the century when Zionism emerged
as an ideology and a political movement, and the voluntary and nonsovereign nature of both the World Zionist
Organization and the Jewish institutions in Palestine.
The visions of the main Zionist movements constituted
all-encompassing world views which conflicted with one
another. Labor had a universalistic, social democratic
ideology which emphasized pioneering, settlement of the
land, and egalitarianism. Labor's leaders perceived
the militaristic, militant nationalism of the Revisionists as fascist. Revisionism was strongly influenced
by Polish nationalism and stressed "blood and iron,"
the values of martial heroism. The Revisionists were
convinced that Labor's universalism was assimilationist
and feared its links with communism. The policies of
the two regarding the partition of Palestine, attitudes
toward the Arabs, and relations with the British Mandatory regime were contradictory.[2]

 During bitter rhetorical exchanges, Ben-Gurion
called the Revisionists fascists, referred to his rival
Jabotinsky as "Il Duce" (Mussolini's title), and compared him to Hitler (prior to the Holocaust). The Revisionists responded in kind by referring to Ben-Gurion
as "a British agent" and called the Laborites "Bolshe-
viks." Emotions reached a peak on June 16, 1933, when
the prominent labor leader Chaim Alosoroff was murdered

and two members of an extremist faction of the Revisionists were charged with the crime. Although there
was insufficient evidence to convict them, the incident
cast a cloud of suspicion which was sufficiently salient to prompt Menachem Begin to appoint a government
commission of inquiry to investigate the murder fifty
years later.[3]

During the tense atmosphere created by the bitter
rivalry between the two largest political movements in
the Yishuv (the Jewish community in Palestine), their
leaders, Ben-Gurion and Jabotinsky, met secretly in a
series of meetings in London during October 1934. The
two great rivals agreed to eliminate violence and to
regulate the relations between the trade unions of the
two movements. However, the agreement on cooperation
between the two trade unions met with strong opposition
from both movements. It was defeated in a referendum
held by the Histadrut (General Federation of Labor) on
March 24, 1935. Menachem Begin was among the followers
of Jabotinsky who most strongly opposed the cooperative
agreement with Labor. At a Revisionist World Conference in Cracow in January 1935 Begin told Jabotinsky:
"You may forget, sir, that Ben-Gurion called you Vladimir Hitler. But our memories are better."[4]

One important factor which significantly influenced the nature and the outcome of the competition
between the two major movements was Jabotinsky's decision to lead his Revisionists out of the World Zionist
Organization (WZO), and to establish the New Zionist
Organization (NZO) in 1935. In so doing, the Revisionists removed themselves from the most important
international forum in Zionist politics at a critical
formative period. Labor not only benefited by gaining
an increasingly dominant position in the WZO and thus
greater access to its vital resources, but Ben-Gurion
successfully insinuated that the Revisionists had
placed themselves beyond the bounds of mainstream, if
not legitimate, Zionist politics.

The military auxiliaries of the two camps came
precariously close to clashing during the last phase of
the British mandatory rule. Whereas the Haganah, the
main Jewish defense organization led by Ben-Gurion,
practiced a policy of restraint toward the British during World War II, the Irgun Zvai Leumi (National Military Organization, or IZL), led by Begin, pursued an
activist policy directed primarily against the British
presence in Palestine. Lehi (Fighters for Israeli
Freedom), better known as the Stern gang after its commander, Avraham (Yair) Stern, pursued a policy of terrorism and reprisals against both the British and the
Arabs.[5] At one point when Begin and Stern refused to
bring their dissident organizations under the discipline of the elected institutions of the Palestine
Jewish community, Operation Season was implemented.

During this operation elite Palmach units of the Haganah tracked down the dissidents, abducted and interrogated them, occasionally resorting to violence. The British were informed of the names and/or hideouts of some of the dissidents, while in other cases they were even turned over to the British. It has been said that, "for both camps it was the darkest hour in Israel's battle for independence."[6] However, there was an even darker hour yet to follow.

Undoubtedly, the single most serious incident, which brought the conflict between the two camps to the brink of potential civil war, was the Altalena affair. The Altalena, a ship bought by the IZL and loaded with desperately needed arms and ammunition, sailed from Europe to Israel on June 11, 1948. It arrived during a cease-fire arranged by the United Nations. Ben-Gurion had disbanded the military organizations of the pre-state political movements which were in the process of being merged into the newly created Zahal (Israel Defense Forces-IDF). However, the IZL and Lehi maintained their separate and autonomous units in Jerusalem, because the partition plan of the United Nations had declared it to be an international city.

Since Begin had signed an agreement with the provisional government integrating the IZL units into Zahal, Ben-Gurion expected Zahal to receive the Altalena's weapons. When Begin requested that 20 percent of the arms be allocated to IZL units in Jerusalem, his request was granted. But Begin's proposal to use the remaining 80 percent of the weapons exclusively to arm the IZL units within the Israel Defense Forces was rejected, and negotiations between the two sides broke down. The events which followed were the most bitter and the most dangerous in contemporary Israeli history. Their interpretation is colored by the partisan positions of those who discuss the events.[7]

When Begin defied the government's orders to turn over the arms and began unloading the Altalena with the aid of IZL soldiers (many of whom had deserted their Zahal units), a gun battle broke out between the dissidents and government troops. The ship steamed out to sea with Begin on board. The next morning when the Altalena docked at Tel Aviv to unload its cargo the last tragic act of the drama was played out. Hundreds of IZL soldiers and sympathizers had gathered and confronted a much smaller number of Palmach troops commanded by Yigal Allon. The Cabinet had met in an emergency session and decided to demand that the ship be handed over to the government, and to use force if Begin refused. A gun battle broke out between the IZL and Palmach units. A cannon shot struck the ship, a fire broke out, and explosions followed as the ammunition on board was ignited. Fourteen IZL men and one Palmach soldier died and dozens were wounded.

Ben-Gurion and many of the other members of the
government and the army high command feared that the
dissidents would have used the arms from the Altalena
to stage "an armed revolt to seize power or establish a
separate Jewish state in Jerusalem and Judea."[8]   In
fact, Dr. Yisrael Eldad, the leading idealogue of Lehi,
proposed such an idea to Begin during the unloading of
the Altalena, but Begin refused because he was afraid
that this would lead to a civil war.[9]   In retrospect it
is not unlikely that had Begin not demonstrated restraint during this crisis civil war could have been
the consequence.

Even after Israel was established, there were several incidents which challenged the stability of democratic politics.   The most serious of these was the
crisis generated over the agreement between Israel and
the Federal Republic of Germany (with whom Israel had
no formal diplomatic relations), in which Germany
agreed to pay reparations to Israel in compensation for
Jewish property which had been confiscated during the
Third Reich.   There was widespread and highly emotional
opposition to the agreement from both the left-wing and
the right-wing of the Israeli political party spectrum.
On January 7, 1952, the opposition culminated in the
most serious domestic political crisis in Israel since
the Altalena affair.

While Ben-Gurion addressed an extremely tense
Knesset, Menachem Begin addressed a mass rally at a
square a few hundred yards from the legislature.   In a
highly emotional speech Begin referred to his restraint
during the Altalena affair, and threatened that on this
occasion he would show no such restraint saying, "When
you fired at us with cannon, I gave an order: No!
Today, I shall give the order yes!   This will be a battle of life and death."[10]   He continued, "According to
reports we have just received, Mister Ben-Gurion has
stationed policemen armed with grenades and tear gas
made in Germany--the same gas that suffocated our parents."[11]   Declaring his willingness to be sent to concentration camps and to suffer torture chambers, and
with the cry of "Freedom or death!" Begin marched off
to the Knesset with the mob following him.

The impassioned mob broke through the police bar-
ricades, and threw stones at the Knesset breaking many
windows.   Tear gas and the shouts of the angry mob
entered the Knesset chambers through the broken windows.   When the Speaker of the Knesset attempted to
prevent Begin from speaking from the podium during the
debate, Begin is reported to have said, "If I don't
speak, no one shall speak!"[12]   Ben-Gurion was forced to
call in the army to restore order on the grounds and in
the vicinity of the Knesset.   In a radio broadcast to
the nation the next day Ben-Gurion condemned Begin for
having attempted to destroy democracy in Israel.   This

incident contributed to Ben-Gurion's success in projecting an image of Begin and his followers as irresponsible and on the fringe, if not beyond the limits,
of legitimate political activity.

It is generally, although not unanimously, agreed
among experts on Israeli politics that in the process
of establishing Labor's political and ideological dominance and legitimacy during the critical formative
stages of the development of the society and the state,
Ben-Gurion (and other leaders of the Labor movement)
succeeded in delegitimizing the Revisionists, IZL, and
the post-Independence Herut party led by Begin.
Clearly their ideological world views were poles apart
and there was considerable personal antipathy between
the leaders of the two movements. For example,
Ben-Gurion repeatedly refused Begin's requests to honor
Jabotinsky's will which requested that his remains
(which were buried in the United States where
Jabotinsky died in 1940) be reburied by the sovereign
Jewish government in Israel. Even as late as a Knesset
debate on May 13, 1963 (a month prior to his
resignation as prime minister), Ben-Gurion expressed
his obsessive anxiety that if Begin's Herut was to come
to power, "he will replace the army and policy command
with his ruffians and rule the way Hitler ruled
Germany, using brute force to suppress the labor
movement; and will destroy the state." [13]

Also, by declaring that all political parties were
considered to be legitimate potential coalition partners except Maki (Communist) and Herut, Ben-Gurion en-
sured the centrality and dominance of his own Labor
party (Mapai). Therefore, the exclusion of Herut was a
most effective political strategy, since it made it
impossible to form a coalition government without
Mapai. A combination of personal, ideological, and
practical considerations appear to have influenced
Ben-Gurion's policy of politically isolating Herut.

Given the dynamic growth in population, which included immigrants from practically every nation in the
world, and substantial changes in crucial aspects of
the economy, society, and culture, significant political changes were inevitable. In fact what is surprising is not that Labor lost its ideological and political dominance, but that it took almost fifty years to
do so. I have attempted to show how changes in the
society related to internal dynamics within the party;
and I have argued that just as Labor gained ideological
dominance before it achieved a dominant position in the
political system, the loss of ideological hegemony preceded the party's fall from power in 1977. [14]

"Normalization"

During the period in which Labor's paramount position was being eroded, a parallel process took place
through which Herut gradually overcame its isolation
and pariah status, and gained increasing legitimacy.
Levite and Tarrow have analyzed the strategies pursued
by Herut to attain this goal.[15] By the mid-1950s, Herut
began modifying its free enterprise-oriented socioeconomic platform with a greater openness to welfare
programs in order to broaden their electoral appeal.

When Levi Eshkol became prime minister after the
resignation of Ben-Gurion in 1963, he acceded to the
request to rebury the remains of Jabotinsky in Israel
in defiance of his former mentor's strong objections.
The state funeral for the late Revisionist leader on
Mount Herzl, at a site reserved for the great leaders
of the nation, symbolized the beginning of the process
through which his disciples and followers attained
legitimate status.

During its seventh party conference in 1963, Herut
made a historic decision. It decided to join the Labor
dominated Histadrut in order to undermine it from within. Mapai managed to block these efforts through legal
battles until 1965, when Herut formed an electoral
alignment with the Liberal party, called Gahal, and, in
this new form, competed in both the Histadrut and the
Knesset elections in the same year. The asssociation
with the Liberals gave Herut new respectability and
paved the way for the next and most crucial stage of
the legitimization of Herut--its first participation in
government.

The most significant act of political legitimization came during the extremely tense period prior to
the outbreak of the war of June 1967 when pressures
within the Labor party and the coalition and from public opinion resulted in the inclusion of Gahal in a
broadly based Government of National Unity. The
responsible participation of Menachem Begin and the
other Gahal members in close cooperation with Labor
until 1970, well beyond the immediate national
emergency of the 1967 War, conclusively established
Begin's credentials and the legitimacy of his party for
many Israelis.

In addition to establishing a responsible image
through participation in the Government of National
Unity, a number of additional factors contributed to
the increasing legitimization of the Herut wing of
Gahal. Demographic trends worked in their favor. The
increasing proportion of younger voters, who were not
influenced by the earlier period of intense conflict
between the two movements, supported Gahal in greater
numbers than did their parents. This was particularly
the case for the second generation of Jews from the

Islamic countries of North Africa and the Middle East,
who, with their parents, now constitute a majority of
the population. The debacle associated with the initial stages of the surprise attacks from Egypt and
Syria that launched the 1973 War further undermined
public confidence in Labor and worked to the advantage
of the opposition. Labor began to look less invinci-
ble, and the opposition broadened its support by re-
cruiting popular generals and other groups with the
formation of the Likud in 1973.

The success of Gahal in 1967 resulted in the occupation of territories, particularly the West Bank of
the Jordan river, the Biblical Judea and Samaria, which
made manifest ideological issues which had not been
salient since Israel's borders were determined by the
1948 armistice agreements. It raised fundamental questions relating not only to territorial boundaries, but
also to the very character and meaning of the state.

> Since the Six-Day War...we have come to realize
> that questions we thought decided were not de-
> cided.... The political debate on the future of
> the territories in western Eretz Israel occupied
> in the war became no more than a chink through
> which the depths of controversy and interpreta-
> tion, intention and fantasy...were exposed once
> again.[16]

Renewed Polarization

The crisis of identity which characterized various
segments of Israeli society, after a lengthy gestation
period following the 1967 war, was born in the after-
math of the war in 1973. Many of the old symbols and
myths lost their meaning for many people, and new ones
arose to take their place. One striking characteristic
was the increasing penetration of religious symbolism
in what, according to some scholars, constitutes a New
Civil Religion or a New Zionism, one based on a nonrational mythical or totemic world view.[17]

The acquisition of the territories also resulted
in diametrically opposed perceptions of the nature of
the threat to national survival which had serious
political consequences. "Once the threat is different-
ly perceived, it pits against each other those who
identify different--often contradictory--ways of meeting perceived dangers."[18]

The Likud's position with regard to the importance of these territories complemented the ideology of
the increasingly influential leaders of the young
generation of the National Religious Party (NRP or
Mafdal). The educational institutions of the NRP
also spawned Gush Emunim (Bloc of the Faithful), a

religious-political movement with a messianic mission
dedicated to settling Judea and Samaria and incorporat-
ing them into the state of Israel. Gush Emunim arose
within the ideological vacuum created by the loss of
Labor dominance, almost as a response to it. The movement challenged and helped to undermine both the authority of the Labor government--through demonstrations, illegal settlements, and confrontations with the
army when it was sent to remove them from sites on
which they had squatted--and the ideological supremacy
of Labor, which was already very much on the wane, by
claiming to be the true heirs of pioneering Zionism.
The Likud coopted Gush Emunim and utilized it as an
ideological vanguard through which it increased the
legitimacy of its policies.[19]

It is in terms of these important cultural changes
that the political developments including the renewal
and intensification of polarization must be understood.
Weissbrod argues that, "If the Likud wanted to be recognized as the political center of Israel, New Zionism
had to become the dominant ideology and Likud the dominant party."[20] The attempt by the Likud to establish
both political and ideological dominance since its
ascendance to power in the government is a key factor
in explaining the renewed polarization, as was, to a
lesser extent, the ineffectual and occasionally exaggerated response of the Labor party to this challenge.

Although Golda Meir had collaborated with Menachem
Begin in governments of national unity, as late as February 24, 1974, she warned her colleagues in a meeting
of the Labor Party Central Committee that, "I do not
doubt that if the Government would be led by the Likud,
it would be a national disaster."[21] In the election
campaign of 1977, Labor used scare tactics which attempted to convince the public of the dire consequences
of a Likud victory. These tactics were ineffective, if
not counterproductive, because they lacked credibility
among much of the general public.

Yet, the unanticipated Likud victory created a
climate of uncertainty and anxiety among wide sectors
of the public which was expressed in editorials in
major newspapers. The Likud sought to assuage these
anxieties through newspaper notices which promised, "We
shall protect the State of Israel to the utmost."[22]
The climate of public anxiety undoubtedly influenced
Prime Minister Begin's selection of his cabinet, particularly his choice of Moshe Dayan as foreign minister.
Begin's appointment of the former Labor defense minister, whom he greatly respected, provided a symbol of
continuity with past governments through which he hoped
to derive additional legitimacy, and it signaled the
relative "moderation" of his new cabinet. The same
objectives were achieved through the retention of civil
servants, including many in top positions who had

served previous administrations.[23]   Similarly, the
Likud government moved slowly in making substantive
changes in domestic policy.[24]   The most significant
achievement of the first Likud government, the successful conclusion of the historic peace treaty with Egypt,
received stronger backing from the Labor benches in the
Knesset than from Begin's own party.   This achievement
was possibly more popular among those who had been most
anxious about the election of the Likud than among
those who had most strongly supported Begin throughout
the years.

Why then was the 1981 Israeli election campaign
the most violent in decades?   Clearly, one of the major
reasons was its close outcome.   It was the first election in Israeli history in which the result was not
presumed to be known in advance.   In the previous election, most people (including pollsters and political
scientists) wrongly assumed that the Labor Party would
be victorious.   In 1977, victors and losers alike were
shocked at the election results.   In 1981, as Israelis
went to the polls most pollsters and pundits predicted
the election could go either way.   This was a formi-
dable accomplishment for the Likud since the cabinet
had been significantly altered by the resignations of
Moshe Dayan from the foreign ministry in October 1979,
Ezer Weizmann from the defense ministry at the end of
May 1980, and both Simcha Ehrlich and Yigal Hurvitz
from the finance ministry as Israel's triple-digit inflation became the second highest in the world.   In
fact, between October 1980 and January 1981, public
opinion polls predicted that the Labor party would receive an unprecedented absolute majority of 61 of the
Knesset's 120 seats compared to the Likud's predicted
29 seats.

The early predictions that Labor would return to
power made its leaders overconfident, and aroused anxiety in the ranks of the Likud.   Begin had alienated
some of his most ardent supporters by returning the
Sinai to the Egyptians and, in so doing, "uprooting"
Jewish settlements, a euphemism which gained wide use.
He was particularly anxious for another term of office
in order to implement his plans for the massive Jewish
settlement of Judea and Samaria which he was confident
would preclude the return of these territories to Arab
sovereignty by any future Labor government.   Given his
vision of the historic importance of this mission,
Begin and his closest colleagues were motivated to win
the elections at practically any cost.   Analysis of the
Likud's electoral strategy and tactics, and particularly of Begin's rhetorical style and the symbolic themes
which he invoked, indicates that these factors played a
key role in the renewal of political polarization and
the escalation of violence which characterized the campaign and the period that followed.

The Likud is by no means solely responsible for
the political violence. Nor did it bear primary responsibility for the underlying socio-cultural and
political tensions. However, the Likud both expressed
and exploited deep-seated underlying feelings of
frustration, resentment, and even hatred among certain
sectors of the electorate. Since Labor dominated the
Israeli political system for nearly fifty years, it was
credited with many of the achievements of the state,
but was also blamed for many failures. Labor neither
deserved all of the credit it claimed nor all of the
blame it received from its opponents. Begin, a master
of rhetorical skills, successfully articulated the
feelings of those who had been excluded from the main
centers of power and from the centers of social, cultural, and ideological acceptability (or legitimacy in
some cases) during Labor's long reign--his own followers from the Revisionists and Herut, the Oriental or
Eastern Jews, and to a certain extent the religious
Jews.

Labor's self-image as a pioneering vanguard came
to be viewed as elitist arrogance by many who were excluded from the center or were on its margins.[25] If
America was the melting pot, Labor made Israel a pressure cooker in which the immigrants would be blended to
produce a new Israel created in Labor's European image.
Arnold Lewis perceptively captures the essence of the
paternalistic aspects of Labor's approach to the
"absorption of immigrants" in his analysis of folk concepts such as "primitive," the "Desert Generation,"
"Second Israel," "Levantinization," and "those in need
of fostering."[26] He relates these metaphors of social
inequality and their impact on the collective dignity
of the Eastern Jews to the pattern of Labor ideological
and political dominance, in which ethnic politics was
contained and constrained. The defeat of Labor and the
rise of the Likud is significant not only because it
increases the importance of the Eastern vote in the
more competitive system, but also because it allows the
Eastern Jews to redefine their collective status in
Israeli society. Moshe Shokeid critically evaluates an
example of such collective redefinition in the attempt
by a Sephardi intellectual to create a new ethnic myth
aimed at legitimizing the rise to power of this formerly marginal social group.[27]

Labor's version of the Zionist interpretation of
reality is no longer taken for granted. The definition
of ethnic cleavages in cultural terms, a central assumption in Labor's ideology, has been successfully
challenged. By emphasizing dedication to the struggle
for the Land of Israel through Jewish settlement and
annexation of the Golan and the West Bank rather than
socio-cultural characteristics, Begin has offered the
Eastern Jews an effective means through which they can

redefine their collective status and, with him, move
from the margins to the center of Israeli society.
Lewis argues the Eastern Jews have traded support for
the Likud's foreign policy position for symbolic gains
on the domestic front; and he suggests that this
alliance may be a transient phase in the developing
Israeli political system.

It was not the intellectual appeal of Jabotinsky's
ideology which attracted the massive and enthusiastic
support that was expressed for Begin during the election campaign. Whereas Shimon Peres, Labor's candidate
for prime minister, primarily appealed to the voter's
reason, Begin appealed to emotions, particularly patri-
otism and feelings of social and ethnic discrimination.[28] On several occasions, Labor played directly
into his hands. For example, two days before the election at a mass rally in Tel Aviv, the master of cere-
monies, Dudu Topaz, a popular entertainer, made a remark about the "chahchahim" (a derogatory euphemism for
Moroccans), supporters of the Likud, who he said serve
as noncommissioned officers in service units in the
army while the supporters of Labor serve as officers in
combat units. The next day at the same spot at a Likud
mass rally, Begin responded by shouting, "Ashkenazi?!
Sephardi?! Jew!!!" which precipitated a wildly enthusiastic response from his supporters.[29]

On another occasion, the prominent Israeli writer,
A. B. Yehoshua, referred to supporters of Begin who
were engaging in violence against the Labor candidates
and supporters as a mob (asafsuf). Begin responded by
sarcastically referring to the supporters of Labor as
yafeh nefesh. This means literally "beautiful souls"
but can be translated as "bleeding hearts." It was
generally used by Begin (and others) to emphasize the
elitism and the perceived "knee-jerk liberalism" of the
Labor camp.

Begin was particularly effective in using such
rhetorical techniques to appeal to Eastern, traditional, and religious Jews in their own codes; by making
his symbolic references meaningful to their experi-
ences. The prime minister successfully projected his
image as a proud, but humble Jew, a man who shared
their reverence for Jewish tradition. Begin even
managed to maintain his populist antiestablishment
image while he was prime minister. Just as he defied
the arrogant Labor establishment at home, he stood up
to the anti-Semites and enemies of Israel abroad. When
he linked the two he ignited the flames of hatred and
violence. The central theme of "the few against the
many" or "them" against "us" was used by Begin to play
on the national insecurity which for some Israelis approaches paranoia.[30] Begin's rhetorical style frequently relied on the use of such techniques as argument by enthymeme, in which propositions are left

implicit or assumed, thereby enabling him to mobilize
shared sentiments having high emotional charge.[31]   When
Begin charged that Labor's "Jordanian option" would
lead to an "Arafatist state" in several major campaign
speeches, he implied that Labor endangered the very
survival of Israel.[32]

In some cases, the exploitation of resentment led
to overt acts. For example, local Likud leaders
adapted a cartoon depicting subhuman, gorilla-like
thugs (which had originally been labeled with the names
of Arab terrorist organizations) threatening the development town of Kiryat Shmona by relabeling it "Kibbutz Movement - Alignment." They labeled the pack of
rapacious wolves bearing down on the town with the
names of neighboring kibbutzim.[33]   Shortly thereafter,
Peres, the head of Labor's Knesset list, was prevented
from speaking in Kiryat Shmona by Likud supporters
chanting "Begin! Begin!" He was bombarded by tomatoes
and was subjected to obscene gestures. Peres aggra-
vated the situation by condemning the obscene gestures
calling them "Oriental movements." When Peres returned
to the town two years later, he was again prevented
from speaking by an unruly mob of hecklers.

There were many incidents in which Labor rallies
were heckled or broken up, cars bearing Labor bumper
stickers were vandalized, and a branch of the Labor
party was set afire. It is likely not a coincidence
that most cases of violence were directed against
Labor, and that the Likud and other parties were rarely
the targets of such acts. When such acts occurred they
were almost invariably directed against parties to the
left of the Likud such as several threats to bomb the
offices of the liberal Change party. Yossie Sarid, one
of the most outspoken doves in Labor, received repeated
threats on his life.

Two leading members of the Likud national election
staff (both of whom are ranking members of the Knesset)
told me that whereas they felt that the Likud benefited
from the political polarization which characterized the
1981 election campaign, they felt that the physical
violence damaged the party's image. One, who for many
years was in charge of the Organization Department of
Herut, claimed that they made serious efforts to prevent their supporters from engaging in acts of violence
and vandalism, but the situation had gotten out of hand
and was beyond their control. He gave as one example,
the order to the local branch of the party in Kiryat
Shmona not to interfere with the appearance of Peres at
a Labor rally in town a year after the election. The
order was disregarded. He remarked ruefully that research had shown a loss in electoral support, particularly among older voters, due to their association with
the acts of violence.

The new Likud-dominated coalition formed after the election in 1981 was even more ideologically homogeneous and militant than was its predecessor, from which the moderate ministers (Dayan and Weizman) had resigned. The second Likud government pursued with a single-minded purposefulness the policy of settling Jews in new settlements in the territories. Among the more ardent, this bordered on obsessiveness. Settlement was given the highest priority and received far more attention and resources than any item on the government's agenda with the exception of national security. For this government, the issue of Jewish settlement, in what they term Judea and Samaria and which they perceive as the heart of the Land of Israel, was inseparably linked with national security. These policies were vigorously opposed by many leaders of the parliamentary opposition as well as the nonparliamentary peace movement led by Peace Now. The conflict over this highly divisive issue perpetuated the polarization and tensions which had arisen during the election campaign.

The expansion of the war which the government launched against the Palestinian bases in Lebanon beyond their initially announced goals added yet another dimension to the divisive political debate in Israel. The unprecedented lack of consensual support for this war dramatically expressed the polarized ideological perceptions of reality held by many Israelis. As Lilly Weissbrod argues, the protest against this war was particularly noteworthy because it was the first time that any significant part of the Israeli public questioned the justice of an Israeli war, especially during the initial victorious stages.[34]

Weissbrod correctly contends that the activities of dissident groups like Yesh Gvul (There is a Limit) and Soldiers Against Silence, while limited in support, more profoundly challenged the legitimacy of the Likud government and its policies than the more widely backed protest activities of such groups as Peace Now. I differ with her interpretation of the extremely limited nature of the protest activities. My field work on the protest activities of the peace movement, which focused primarily, although not exclusively, on Peace Now, convinces me that the main thrust of their protest extended considerably beyond censorship of specific persons in the government (such as Minister of Defense Ariel "Arik" Sharon), or policies relating exclusively to the war in Lebanon.[35] Weissbrod tends to exaggerate the extent to which the Likud has achieved acceptance of the legitimacy of its ideology as opposed to acceptance of the legality of its rule. I shall elaborate on this point below.

Whereas Peace Now is an amorphous political movement drawing together people with a variety of

political viewpoints, the vast majority of leaders and
activists at different levels with whom I spoke indicated their strong disagreement with the settlement
policies of the government. They feel these policies
threaten both the Jewish and the democratic character
of Israel by imposing its rule on one million Palestinian Arabs. They also strongly opposed the trend
toward religious nationalism represented in the New
Zionism (or civil religion) of the government and its
supporters. They desired not only to replace the
government, but to change the direction in which society and culture have been moving in recent years. In
fact, most of the top leaders with whom I spoke had
considerable sympathy for the main criticisms of the
government by the dissidents with whom they differed
more in style than substance. The main substantive
difference was that the leaders of Peace Now rejected
the dissidents' policy of refusing to serve in Lebanon
when called up by the army.

The Likud government has not acquired anywhere
near the unquestioned legitimacy that Labor had during
its long dominance. All of the public opinion data
which Weissbrod cites to illustrate the increase in
religiosity, support for settlement in the territories,
and for the war in Lebanon, also clearly show that a
very significant proportion of the Israeli people do
not share these views. Although the polls vary according to how the questions are phrased and when they are
asked, the population is divided fairly equally over
many of the most pressing questions facing the nation
today. The Likud government acts as if it has the
overwhelming mandate of legitimacy which is derived
from ideological hegemony. By pursuing highly controversial policies that are vehemently opposed by significant sectors of the society, including most of the
intellectuals and the media, it contributed directly to
the intensification of polarization.[36]

Although the Labor opposition supported the goal
of driving Palestine Liberation Organization (PLO)
forces from artillery range of Israel's northern
border, the original reason given by the government for
launching the "Peace for Galilee" war, Labor became increasingly critical as the government expanded the
scope of the war beyond 45 kilometers. For example,
Labor cosponsored (with Peace Now and two small parliamentary parties) the rally which demanded that the
government appoint a commission of inquiry to investigate the massacre in the Sabra and Shatila refugee
camps. The rally was the largest in Israeli history
with approximately 400,000 participants. This led to
the accusation by Prime Minister Begin that Labor was
aiding the enemies of Israel through irresponsible
criticism. Members of the ruling coalition were quick
to point out that they had never criticized the

government during previous wars when they were in the
opposition. Obviously Labor, as a party to the left of
the government, was more vulnerable to such charges
than were the constituent parties of the Likud, all of
whom are to the right of Labor.

Some of Begin's less judicious supporters in the
Knesset went even farther and charged that the opponents of the war were traitors. One deputy minister
told me that such critics in the opposition were not
only disloyal to the government, but were traitors to
the Jewish people. The consistent repetition of such
charges, and use of the terms traitor (bogade), fifth
column, knife in the back of the nation, and supporter
of the PLO (Ashafist) indicated a policy which aimed to
make criticism of the government and its policies ille-
gitimate. Such attempts to delegitimize opposition can
be seen as part of the Likud's effort to establish its
political and ideological dominance.

In a Knesset debate on September 22, 1982, over
the proposal to establish a government commission of
inquiry to investigate the massacre in the Sabra and
Shatila refugee camps in Lebanon, Begin taunted the
Labor benches saying, "Nobody is afraid of your threats
of civil war." He was evidently referring to a newspaper interview in which A. B. Yehoshua (who holds no
position in the Labor party) had expressed his fear of
the possibility of civil war. Begin went on to personally attack Peres for exploiting the catastrophe when
a "blood libel" had been made against Israel.

The opposition frequently countered such charges
by accusing the government of demagoguery. The more
leftist Knesset members, especially the communists,
consistently called the government fascist. The leaders of the Labor party usually used terms like neo-
fascist or Peronist when describing the Likud government. Whereas many (although not all) Knesset members
could "frame" such name-calling in its "proper" context, and drink coffee with political opponents after
parliamentary debates (several indicated to me that it
had become increasingly difficult to do so), some of
their less politically sophisticated militant supporters tended to take such charges more literally. If the
opponents of the war aided the enemy, they deserved to
be beaten up. If they were traitors, they deserved
worse.

On February 10, 1983, Peace Now organized a march
from downtown Jerusalem to the Prime Minister's office
to demand that the government fully implement the recommendations of the Kahan Commission Report on the massacres of Palestinians in the refugee camps of Sabra
and Shatila by Christian Lebanese forces. The peaceful
marchers were jeered and taunted with all of the afore-
mentioned epithets. They were pushed, punched, spat
upon, and rocks were thrown at them. The number of

police present was woefully inadequate to contain the aggressive hecklers. At the prime minister's office, there were speeches by Peace Now leaders, and the demonstration concluded with the singing of HaTikva (the Hope), Israel's national anthem. As the crowd was dispersing, a hand grenade was thrown, killing Emile Grunzweig, and wounding several others including the son of Cabinet Minister Yosef Burg. Media reports that groups of young thugs had harassed those who brought the wounded to the hospital could not be positively confirmed, but it was verified that several top leaders of Peace Now were assaulted at one hospital when they went to visit the wounded.

The following evening television news carried alternating pictures of the thousands of mourners at the funeral of Emile Grunzweig, and of Defense Minister Sharon speaking at the association of lawyers where he attacked the Kahan Commission Report which had recommended that he be relieved of his cabinet responsibilities. The pictures of Sharon laughing and joking while much of the nation was mourning a young man whose murder they felt symbolized a threat to Israeli democracy, vividly illustrated serious differences in perceptions of reality among some Israelis.

The next Knesset debate illustrated the same point even more elaborately. It was opened by Prime Minister Begin who expressed his sorrow at the death of Emile Grunzweig and condemned violence. He also announced that Sharon had relinquished the defense portfolio, but would remain in the cabinet. There was considerable criticism from the opposition benches by members who claimed that Sharon's retention in the government violated the spirit of the recommendations of the Kahan Commission. In spite of the agreement among the Knesset parliamentary factions to maintain a "cultured" debate and the genuine concern of many Knesset members about the danger signalled by the unprecedented political murder, the debate illustrated greater polarization than reconciliation. Yigal Hurwitz, former Likud minister of the treasury, expressed the feelings of many other politically responsible Knesset members when he warned both sides of the house of the danger of "this crazy polarization."

The cartoonist Jacob Kirschen poignantly summed up the week through his character Shuldig who said:

I've been sick in bed for a week now and I've been tossing and turning and having nightmares. I dreamt we went mad with half of us thinking the other half fascist and the other half thinking that the first half are cowards and traitors. I dreamt about political murder and violent Knesset 'debating' about violent street 'debating'. Phew! I think it's time to stop taking these pills.[37]

President Yitzhak Navon (who had called on the government to appoint the commission of inquiry) warned the nation of the grave implications of the political, ethnic, and religious polarization. He asserted that the violence of language had led to physical violence, and now to murder. Claiming that Israel had reached a critical turning point, Navon stressed the need for tolerance and national unity. In an interview with a French periodical, Navon warned of the possibility of civil war in Israel if the direction of increasing polarization did not change.

Former secretary-general of the Labor party, Arie "Lova" Eliav, claimed that the process which led to the death of Emile Grunzweig began with the occupation of the West Bank. He argued that the increasing expressions of animosity and violence toward Arabs had been transferred to those people who opposed the government's policies and who were considered traitors by the government's most militant supporters. The view that the occupation and the rule over the Palestinian inhabitants of the territories is corrupting the ethical traditions on which Israeli democracy is based is widely held among the opponents of the government's settlement policies, particularly among intellectuals.

These critics cite the increase in vigilantism by Jewish settlers against the Arabs in the territories, as discussed by David Weisburd and Vered Vinitzky, as evidence to support their argument.[38] Weisburd and Vinitzky demonstrate that the settlers of Gush Emunim have developed an ideological legitimization for taking the law into their own hands which has received support from the military authorities. The critics charge that the vigilantes could not possibly succeed in repeatedly breaking the law and getting away unpunished without receiving substantial political support from the highest political echelons. They argue that the encouragement of such acts of violence and disregard for the law corrupts the democratic foundations of the state, and can be directly related to the increase in violence within Israel as well.[39]

Such views, when expressed by opposition politicians, intellectuals, and journalists in editorials of liberal newspapers, are perceived by many ardent supporters of the government's settlement policies as being tantamount to treason. This charge can be heard throughout Israel; in the Knesset members' dining room, in the fruit and vegetable market in Jerusalem, and in the Gush Emunim settlements.[40] For example, on one occasion I went to Hebron with a new reporter from Ha'aretz, an independent newspaper which has frequently criticized the Likud in its editorials. When he introduced himself to leading figures among the Jewish settlers, he was verbally attacked--at times venomously-- by people whom he had never previously met and who had

never read his articles. The fact that he was from
Ha'aretz meant automatically to them that he was the
"enemy." Yet even those people who were most hostile
and refused to grant him an interview, ended up talking
to him, if only to express their contempt for his paper
and the leftist yafeh nefesh whom they considered it to
represent. Almost everywhere one turns one is confronted with a challenge to state one's position; and
once having done so, one becomes either one of "them"
or one of "us." Once the lines are drawn, the polemic
battle begins.

Virginia Dominguez argues that the terms "left"
and "right" are multivocal and multifunctional.[41]
Their shifting referentiality can provide a flexible
means of establishing solidarity and opposition. She
persuasively argues that the meanings of such terms
must be contextually interpreted. Any attempt to
categorize Israeli parties along a simple left-right
continuum seriously distorts the complexity and the
nuances of Israeli politics.

Conclusions

The most recent trend toward reemergent and deep-
ening polarization has the effect of eliminating flexibility, ignoring complexities and nuances by collapsing
the multivalent, and cross-cutting nature of political
divisions in Israel into simple dichotomous categories.
The world is perceived through the prism of binary op-
posites: "them" against "us" or the forces of light
versus the forces of darkness. Paraphrasing Baldwin,
McWilliams points out that in the midst of battle all
people speak in slogans and ignore complexities.[42]

Green stresses that the process of simplification
and polarization of politics preceded and facilitated
the countermobilization leading to the Iranian revolution.[43] McWilliams has observed that, "A house becomes
divided 'against itself' when what is unlike is regarded as more important than what is akin."[44] The
question is whether Israelis are beginning to regard
their political differences as more important than
their shared values and interests.

The reality of Israeli politics is considerably
more complex than the dichotomized perceptions dis-
torted by the process of polarization. Not all observers would agree that polarization has reached such
serious proportions. Compared with the earlier period,
when divisions in the Yishuv and early state period
were more intense and pervasive, the present conflicts
appear to be more superficial, and possibly transient
in nature. Diskin concludes that serious polarization
exists in spite of the absence of extreme ideological
distance between the two camps.[45] On some issues

ideological differences within parties can be as great
as, if not greater than, differences between parties.
In fact the policies of the opposing political blocs
have converged in some areas and are closer than in the
earlier period of conflict. As the two main blocs con-
solidate and converge the remaining differences have
become exaggerated. Strong, nonrational, emotional
responses, feelings of frustration, fear, and resentment, were evoked through the invocation of potent symbolic messages. The particular confluence of circumstances which came together to ignite political pas-
sions in the recent period may very well be a passing
phase in the transition of the political system. The
retirement from active participation in public life of
the leading actor in this phase may possibly augur for
a decline in bitter polemics and polarization.

One of the most important distinguishing features
of Israeli society is that the major social, economic,
and political institutions and certain aspects of the
political culture, were self-consciously created by the
leaders of the dominant voluntary associations of the
Jewish community in Palestine. Many of these pioneering visionaries lived to realize their dream of an independent Jewish state.

A newly created society such as Israel faces particularly acute challenges to the taken-for-grantedness
of its visionary political culture from the generation
which succeeds the founders. This is especially so
when the society undergoes dynamic growth and diversi-
fication of its population and of its social, economic,
and political institutions. Perhaps inevitably, a dis-
parity developed between the changing social reality
and the structure of symbolic meanings that constituted
the dominant socialist version of the Zionist civil
religion. Contradictions became more apparent and were
exploited. With the corruption of previously "sacred"
creeds, a new revitalized alternative interpretation of
Zionist civil religion was adopted by formerly marginal
groups which successfully challenged Labor's dominance.
Their attempt--thus far unsuccessful--to establish
their own ideological hegemony has played a major role
in the recent renewal of polarization.

All societies require a minimal common symbolic
structure of shared meanings in order to function. In
the absence of such a minimal political culture, serious political conflicts may ultimately result in civil
war. Israel appears to have a greater need for a collective vision and a sense of mission than most states,
whose right to exist is taken for granted by their
neighbors and by the international community. The an-
cient myth which proclaims a national mission, that the
Jewish state should be "a light unto the nations," was
incorporated into the most popular versions of Zionism,
secular as well as religious. Horowitz has argued that

given the political and military demands of sovereignty
this goal is unrealistic for a nation state; it invites
the application of a double standard and the hypocriti-
cal criticism of others.[46] The goal and attempt to act
as a moral vanguard contradicts another principal
Zionist objective, to be a normal nation "like all the
nations." Yehoshua recommends that the claim to
"chosenness" be abandoned.[47] That such suggestions
have thus far generally fallen on deaf ears may indicate the continuing salience of this myth in Israeli
political culture.

It is almost as if the very successes of the
Zionist dream in the first three decades of statehood
resulted in disillusionment, because the society had
somehow fallen short of its self-proclaimed utopian
vision as a moral example for the world. The following
passage from Walter Miller's A Canticle for Leibowitz
poignantly expresses such an orientation or condition:

> The closer men came to perfecting for themselves a
> paradise, the more impatient they seemed to become
> of it as it grew in richness and power and beauty;
> for then, perhaps, it was easier for them to see
> that something was missing in the garden, some
> tree or shrub that would not grow. When the world
> was in darkness and wretchedness, it could believe
> in perfection and yearn for it. But when the
> world became bright with reason and riches, it be-
> gan to sense the narrowness of the needle's eye,
> and that rankled for a world no longer willing to
> believe or yearn.[48]

The main difference between Israel and the world
of Miller's novel is that there are many Israelis who
still believe and probably even more who yearn to do
so. The problem, however, is that they no longer appear to believe the same myths, and there is the danger
that eventually they may cease to believe that they
share the same vision and destiny. Whether or not this
happens depends not only on which coalition of parties
will govern for the foreseeable future, but to a large
extent on the quality of leaders which Israel produces
in the immediate future, and whether they are capable
of projecting a vision which the majority of Israelis
share. This vision will have to unite the nation
around a common symbolic framework and at the same time
not further isolate Israel from the rest of the world.
Such a vision will require a creative synthesis of both
the primordial loyalties and universalistic values inherent in traditional Jewish culture which have been
vital aspects of Zionism in the past. Although the
threat of false messianism is no less dangerous than
the cynicism caused by disillusioned idealism, only a
refurbished and strengthened political culture can

provide the essential sense of common vision and destiny which Israel desperately needs to overcome its current crisis of political legitimacy.

Acknowledgments

I am grateful to the Joint Committee on the Near and Middle East of the American Council of Learned Societies and the Social Science Research Council which awarded me a grant from funds provided by the National Endowment for the Humanities and the Ford Foundation, and to Rutgers--the State University of New Jersey, which awarded me a Faculty Academic Study Program leave and grant that enabled me to conduct research in Israel during the year 1982-1983. I wish to sincerely thank the hundreds of politicians, civil servants, educators, religious leaders, cultural figures, members of the media, and Israelis from every walk of life and political persuasion who generously gave their time in conversations with me. I am particularly indebted to Rita Aronoff, Dan Caspi, Irving Louis Horowitz, and Gerald Pomper for their helpful comments on a draft of this essay which was presented at a conference on "Israel After Begin" co-sponsored by the Middle East Institute and The Johns Hopkins School of Advanced International Studies on January 20, 1984. I gratefully acknowledge the valuable editorial comments made by Steven Heydemann for this volume. This essay is a revised version of an earlier paper. Published by permission of Transaction, Inc., from Cross Currents in Israeli Culture and Politics, Political Anthropology, Vol. 4, edited by Myron J. Aronoff, copyright 1984 by Translation, Inc.

NOTES

1. Walter Miller, A Canticle for Leibowitz (New York: Bantam, 1961), p. 273.
2. Rael Jean Isaac, Party and Politics in Israel: Three Visions of a Jewish State (New York: Longman, 1981), p. 41.
3. Shabtai Teveth, Retzach Alozorov [The Alozorov murder] (Jerusalem: Schocken, 1982).
4. Michael Bar-Zohar, Ben-Gurion: A Biography, trans., Peretz Kidron (Jerusalem: Steinmatzky, 1978), p. 73.
5. Joseph B. Schectman and Yehuda Benari, History of the Revisionist Movement (Tel Aviv: Hadar Publishing House, 1970).
6. David Niv, The Irgun Zevai Leumi (Jerusalem: World Zionist Organization Department for Education and Culture, 1980); and Tzvi Tzameret, Lohame Herut Israel

(Lehi) [Israel freedom fighters] (Jerusalem: World Zionist Organization Department for Education and Culture).

7. Eitan Haber, Menachem Begin: The Man and the Legend (New York: Dell, 1978), p. 217.

8. Uri Brenner, Altalena (Tel Aviv: Kibbutz Hameuchad, 1978) [Hebrew]; and Shlomo Nakdimon, Altalena (Jerusalem: Yediot Aharonot, 1978) [Hebrew].

9. Bar-Zohar, Ben-Gurion, p. 171.

10. Reported by Dr. Israel Eldad in a personal interview with the author.

11. Bar-Zohar, Ben-Gurion, p. 197.

12. Ibid.

13. Ibid. and Haber, Menachem Begin, p. 355.

14. Bar-Zohar, Ben-Gurion, p. 303.

15. Myron J. Aronoff, Power and Ritual in the Israel Labor Party: A Study in Political Anthropology (Amsterdam/Assen: Van Gorcum, 1977); Myron J. Aronoff, "The Decline of the Israel Labor Party: Causes and Significance," in Israel at the Polls - 1977, ed. Howard Penniman (Washington, D.C.: American Enterprise Institute Studies in Political and Social Processes, 1979), pp. 114-145; Myron J. Aronoff, "The Labor Party in Opposition," in Israel in the Begin Era, ed. Robert O. Freedman (New York: Praeger, 1982), pp. 76-101.

16. Ariel Levite and Sidney Tarrow, "The Legitimation of Excluded Parties in Dominant Party Systems - A Comparison of Israel and Italy," Comparative Politics 15 (1983), 295-327.

17. A. B. Yehoshua, Between Right & Right: Israel Problem or Solution? trans. Arnold Schwartz (New York: Doubleday, 1981), p. vii.

18. Charles S. Liebman and Eliezer Don-Yehiya, Civil Religion in Israel: Traditional Judaism and Political Culture in the Jewish State (Berkeley: University of California Press, 1983; Charles S. Liebman and Eliezer Don-Yehiya, "The Dilemma of Reconciling Traditional, Cultural, and Political Needs: Civil Religion in Israel," in Religion and Politics, Political Anthropology Volume 3, ed. Myron J. Aronoff (New Brunswick: Transaction, 1984), pp. 47-62; Lilly Weissbrod, "Delegitimation and Legitimation as a Continuous Process: A Case Study of Israel," The Middle East Journal 35 (1981), 527-543; and Robert Paine, "Israel and Totemic Time?" Royal Anthropological Institute News (December 1983).

19. Isaac, Party and Politics in Israel, p. 207.

20. Lilly Weissbrod, "Gush Emunim Ideology - From Religious Doctrine to Political Action," Middle Eastern Studies 18 (1982), 265-275; Aronoff, "Gush Emunim: The Institutionalization of a Charismatic, Messianic, Religious-Political Revitalization Movement in Israel," in Religion and Politics, Political Anthropology,

76

Volume 3, ed. Myron J. Aronoff (New Brunswick: Transaction, 1984), pp. 63-84.

21. Weissbrod, "Delegitimation and Legitimation," p. 539.

22. Aronoff, Power and Ritual, p. 153.

23. Weissbrod, "Delegitimation and Legitimation," p. 535.

24. Efraim Torgovnik, "Likud 1977-81: The Consolidation of Power," in Israel in the Begin Era, ed. Robert O. Freedman (New York: Praeger, 1982), pp. 7-27.

25. Ira Sharkansky and Alex Radian, "Changing Domestic Policy," in Israel in the Begin Era, ed. Robert O. Freedman (New York: Praeger, 1982), pp. 56-75.

26. Myron J. Aronoff, "Labor in Opposition," p. 97.

27. Arnold Lewis, "Ethnic Politics and the Foreign Policy Debate in Israel," in Cross Currents in Israeli Culture and Politics, Political Anthropology, Volume 4, ed. Myron J. Aronoff (New Brunswick: Transaction, 1984).

28. Moshe Shokeid, "A Case of Ethnic Mythmaking," in Cross Currents in Israeli Culture and Politics, Political Anthropology, Volume 4, ed. Myron J. Aronoff (New Brunswick: Transaction, 1984).

29. Haim Yavin, "Al Sidrat Ha 'Nivcharim' B'Televisia: Haya Zeh Mivtza Meshuga," [On the television series the 'Elected': this was a crazy campaign], in Sefer HaShana Shel Haetoni'im 1982 [The 1982 Journalists' Yearbook], ed. Moshe Lehrer (Tel Aviv: The Association of Journalists, 1981), p. 39.

30. Ibid.

31. Nurit Gretz, "Miatim Mool Rabim: Retorika V Mivneh B'neumei Ha Bechirote Shel Menachem Begin" [Few against many: rhetoric and structure in the election speeches of Menachem Begin], Siman Kriah 16-17 (1983), 106-114. Appendix; Menachem Begin's speech at Kikar Malkei Yisrael 6.28.81, pp. 114-126.

32. Robert Paine, ed. Politically Speaking: Cross-Cultural Studies of Rhetoric (Philadelphia: Institute for the Study of Human Issues, 1981), pp. 9-23.

33. Yavin, "The 'Elected'," p. 39.

34. Helga Dudman, "Collective Resentment," The Jerusalem Post, International Edition (July 19-25), p. 14.

35. Lilly Weissbrod, "Protest and Dissidence in Israel," in Cross Currents in Israeli Culture and Politics, Political Anthropology, Volume 4 (New Brunswick: Transaction, 1984).

36. A full analysis of this material and many other issues dealt with in this essay will appear in my forthcoming Israeli Visions and Divisions: Cultural Change and Political Conflict.

37. Jacob Kirschen, "Dry Bones," The Jerusalem Post (February 16, 1983).

38. David Weisburd with Vered Vinitzky, "Vigilant-ism as Rational Social Control: The Case of the Gush Emunim Settlers," in Cross Currents in Israeli Culture and Politics, Political Anthropology, Volume 4, ed. Myron J. Aronoff (New Brunswick: Transaction, 1984).

39. The main theme of the annual meeting of the Israel Criminological Association held at Haifa University on May 5-6, 1983 was "Violence in Israeli Society." The increase in violence in various spheres of Israeli society was extensively discussed.

40. Amos Oz, In the Land of Israel, trans. Maurie Goldberg-Bartura (New York: A Helen and Kurt Wolff Book, Harcourt Brace Jovanovich, 1983).

41. Virginia R. Dominguez, "The Language of Left and Right in Israeli Politics," in Cross Currents in Israeli Culture and Politics, Political Anthropology, Volume 4, ed. Myron J. Aronoff (New Brunswick: Transaction, 1984).

42. W. Carey McWilliams, "The Bible in the Ameri-can Political Tradition," in Religion and Politics, Political Anthropology, Volume 3, ed. Myron J. Aronoff (New Brunswick: Transaction, 1984), p. 34.

43. Jerrold D. Green, "Religion and Countermobili-zation in the Iranian Revolution," in Religion and Politics, Political Anthropology, Volume 3, ed. Myron J. Aronoff (New Brunswick: Transaction, 1984), pp. 85-104.

44. McWilliams, "The Bible in the American Politi-cal Tradition," p. 31.

45. Avraham Diskin, "Polarization and Volatility Among Voters," in The Roots of Begin's Success: The 1981 Israeli Elections, eds. Dan Caspi, Avraham Diskin, and Emanuel Gutmann (New York: St. Martin's 1983), pp. 113-140.

46. Irving Louis Horowitz, Israeli Ecstasies/ Jewish Agonies (New York: Oxford University Press, 1974), p. 120.

47. Yehoshua, Between Right & Right, pp. 63-64.

48. Miller, A Canticle for Leibowitz, pp. 235-36.

6
The West Bank and Gaza
in Israeli Politics

Ian S. Lustick

    Few would disagree that the question of the permanent disposition of the West Bank and Gaza Strip is the issue which divides Israelis more seriously than any other. At stake are the territorial extent of the state (the West Bank and Gaza represent approximately 21 percent of Israel's pre-1967 land area), the ethnonational homogeneity of the country, the chances for reaching peace agreements with Arab countries besides Egypt, the possibility of breaking out of the international pariahood stemming from the continuing occupation of these areas, the psychological if not military assets which these territories represent from a security point of view, and the ideological commitments which large numbers of Israelis maintain toward the establishment of Jewish sovereignty over all the "Land of Israel." No other issue has so shaken Israeli society for so long a time, and no issue has presented the Jewish community of Israel with choices which divide it on such basic principles. Nor has there been any other issue in relation to which the hostility of more Israeli Jews to other Israeli Jews has been so intense. Some intra-Jewish violence has already occurred, including a grenade attack on a Peace Now demonstration in February 1983 that left one dead and eight wounded.
    Yet for all its importance, the future of the West Bank has yet to crystallize as the focus of a national election campaign. Four parliamentary elections have been held in Israel since the 1967 war. Not one of them witnessed a full dress debate on the issue of what to do with the territories. Nor was the outcome of any one of them determined by stands taken on this issue. In 1977 corruption in the Labor party, and a general desire to "throw the rascals out," overshadowed what were known to be divergent views of the Labor and Likud parties toward the West Bank and Gaza. In 1981, in spite of the country's economic distress, which was the dominant concern in the minds of most voters, somewhat more attention was paid to the issue. But in the final

79

weeks of the campaign the public was distracted by
bombing raids on Beirut and Baghdad and massive government giveaway programs.

One reason why the Israeli electoral system has
not provided a mechanism for debate and decision on the
issue of the occupied territories is that each of the
major parties in Israel has been seriously divided
on what to do with the West Bank and Gaza. Herut and
Tehiyya on the extreme right, and Shelli, the Movement
for Civil Rights, and the Communist Party on the extreme left, have much more clearly defined positions.
Thus preservation of party unity has often depended on
preventing the emergence of political situations that
would require clear stands to be taken. Indeed it is
the failure of Israeli political parties to express
effectively the intensity and variety of viewpoints
that exist on this issue that helps explain the emergence of powerful extra-party political movements such
as Gush Emunim and Peace Now.

But gradually, political competition in Israel is
beginning to reflect the constellation of Israeli
opinion on the greatest question before the country.
This process has been encouraged by the implementation
of Likud policies designed to eliminate all options
except those acceptable to the extreme right, and by
the traumatic events and losses of the Lebanon War--a
"campaign" portrayed by Defense Minister Ariel Sharon,
Chief of Staff Rafael Eitan and other government leaders, as a struggle for Judea and Samaria.[1] Indeed for
increasing numbers of Israelis the future of the West
Bank and Gaza has become much more than a political
problem. It has rather assumed the proportions of a
fundamental contest over the meaning and purpose of
Zionism, the values Israeli society will live by, and
the terms upon which an accommodation with the Arab
world could ever be realized.

The Terms of the Debate

The terms of the debate in Israel over the future
of the territories were appropriately and eloquently
adumbrated in speeches which Prime Minister Begin and
opposition Labor party Chief Shimon Peres delivered on
October 18, 1982, at the session of the Knesset con-
vened immediately following the end of the Lebanon War.[2]
Both Begin and Peres depicted the choice facing Israel
as one which presents the country with a decision of
destiny. For Begin the choice was between "the integrity of the Land of Israel or its redivision." He
dismissed the idea of territorial compromise associated
with the creation of a Jordanian-Palestinian federation
as "bizarre," "foolish," and as, in fact, equivalent to
the establishment of a PLO-led Palestinian state. He

reminded the Knesset of the traditional debate within
the Zionist movement between those who insist on establishing and maintaining Jewish sovereignty over all
Eretz Yisrael, and those willing, for political or
other reasons, to accept partition of the Land.

> Indeed, not for the first time in our genera-
> tion, each camp will present its arguments and try
> to convince the others of their justness. Similar
> discussions, though not identical, have been con-
> ducted since the Peel Commission plan was raised
> and fell, since the (United Nations) plan was
> drafted and not carried out and since the drafting
> and pigeonholing of the Rogers Plan.

For Begin the outcome of this debate will determine whether Israel lives in security, in all the "land
of our forefathers [which] we shall bequeath, beautiful, fruitful, built up and green to our sons after us,
from generation to generation"; or whether, by removing
"Judea, Samaria, and the Gaza District" from Israel's
control, a PLO-Palestinian state will be established.
Begin predicted that in the event such a state emerges,
the Israeli army would manage to preserve Israel's existence, but at the cost of another war.
Like Begin, Peres also characterized the problem
of the West Bank and Gaza as a profound choice between
two fundamentally different paths. He also excluded
the emergence of a "PLO state" in the territories. But
unlike Begin he envisioned the possibility of a compromise with Jordan and the Palestinians that would
result in Israeli withdrawal from the territories.
Peres described the choice as one betwen a "truly realistic path" involving "negotiations with Jordan--nego-
tiations which will free the Palestinians from our rule
and which are likely to ensure Israel's security
needs"; and a "false and rhetorical Zionism" that will

> lead Israel into the worst place it can be led, to
> the end of its being the state of the Jews, a Jew-
> ish state, with moral values...into a country sunk
> in a dispute without end, when a population is
> growing in it which by its mere existence will
> shake the foundations of the Jewish and Zionist
> being.

Thus while Begin anchored his position in the historical right of the Jewish people to the whole land of
Israel, Peres stressed the demographic problems associated with absorbing 1.4 million more Arabs and the
moral and social problems associated with controlling
or expelling them.
Peres's concerns were dismissed by Begin as "false
realism." An Arab minority, even a large Arab minority,

is, in Begin's view, an unavoidable fact of Jewish statehood. If, asked Begin, it is morally acceptable to rule the Arabs of Nazareth, why should it not be as acceptable to rule the Arabs of Bethlehem? The solution, he argued, is not to ignore the historic right of the Jewish people to the Land of Israel, but to organize relations between the Jewish and Arab populations in a way which prevents the Arabs from infringing upon Jewish rule of the country, its resources, and its future.

Peres's response to Begin's emphasis on the Jews' historic rights went beyond the question of demography to focus on the implications of annexation, and whether Israel would ever be able to live at peace with its neighbors.

> The Arab birthrate, between the Jordan and the sea, numbers up to 76,000 children a year today, part of them Israeli citizens in every way, as compared with 70,000 Jewish children. A majority of 6,000 children.... Mr. Menachem Begin claims that the battle is over Eretz Yisrael. I claim that the battle is over the State of Israel...the State of Israel will not be a Jewish state unless a clear Jewish majority is ensured in it. Against your claim that we are ready to give up territory, we claim that you are ready to give up the certainty that Israel will remain a Jewish state. This is worse. De facto annexation also destroys the chance of making peace with the Arabs. How will you make peace? Without the Arabs? I would like for once to understand what you said here today. You promised that the land will be quiet for 40 years. How? Two sides are needed for quiet, not just one. Is there even one Arab who will agree to your plan?

Without predicting the quick success of peace negotiations on the basis of the Labor Party--U.S. Government "Jordanian option," Peres did advance a vision of peace involving demilitarized zones, a united Jerusalem, and a series of interim arrangements with Jordan based on substantial Israeli withdrawals from the West Bank and Gaza. Security, rather than ideology, is to be the criterion for evaluating the terms of future agreements. The Arab world, as Peres portrayed it, is a complex melange of contradictory and ambiguous signals, presenting opportunities for peacemaking as well as reasons for vigilance.

Begin's vision of peace, as presented in this speech, was of a prolonged cease-fire, enforced on a hostile Arab world more or less uniformly committed to Israel's dismemberment by the deterrent power of the Israeli military. For Begin, Arab hostility to Israel

is as intense and fundamental as ever, and territorial
compromise to achieve peace would only endanger Israel's security at the expense of the Jewish people's
historic rights. With no Arab country able to threaten
Israel militarily, Begin asked why Israel should even
consider compromise.

> ...given present conditions we are in for a long
> period of peace, whether a contractual or a prac-
> tical one.... Syria will not attack the State of
> Israel.... It knows that its chances to defeat
> Israel are remote. On the contrary, in an aggres-
> sive war against Israel it might come to great
> harm in all respects. Jordan, too, cannot--and,
> as far as we know, does not intend to--attack Is-
> rael. During Operation Peace for Galilee it is-
> sued many cables expressing fear lest we attack
> it...[since] no foreseeable danger of a flare-up
> between Israel and its neighbors is expected....
> [T]he question is: Why should such a peace struc-
> ture be destroyed? Why create new conditions in-
> viting, as it were, bloodshed or war? As a result
> of the government's policy, for the first time
> conditions have been created to maintain peace
> between us and our neighbors on all of Israel's
> borders. Is there any logic to inviting the enemy
> into our own homes to undermine or prevent peace?
> If the plan for establishing a Palestinian state
> in Judea, Samaria, and the Gaza District, coupled
> with a federation between it and the Jordanian
> Government, materialized, we would live by our
> destructive sword. If the conditions created by
> our policy persist, we will live in peace and our
> sword will remain in its sheath.

These are the terms of the debate that has gripped
and will grip Israel for the foreseeable future. Sub-
sidiary themes, in these speeches and in the national
debate, pertain to Israel's international isolation,
its changing relationship with the United States, the
future of Israeli-Egyptian relations, the economic burden of the military and of expansive settlement programs, and the types of policies required to maintain
order in the territories. There are two dimensions of
the problem, however, that were not explicitly addressed in these speeches, and which, despite their obvious
importance, have not become central to the debate in
Israel over the future of the territories. One is the
future of Jerusalem, officially reunited as Israel's
"eternal capital." Its newly drawn municipal borders
encompass a large area of the West Bank, including
within them more than 120,000 Arabs. But the symbolic
significance of Jerusalem for Jews, particularly of the
Old City and the Western Wall which it contains, has
discouraged all but a few Israeli doves from raising

the issue in a way that clearly connects the city's future and the ultimate disposition of the West Bank.

The second key issue that has not surfaced as a focus of systematic debate is the future of the Gaza Strip. With a rapidly growing population that recently passed the half million mark, the crowded Gaza Strip presents Israel, in some ways, with problems that are much starker than those presented by the West Bank. Unlike West Bank Palestinians, Gazans do not hold Jordanian passports. Indeed they hold no citizenship whatsoever. Nor has Egypt expressed any interest in assuming permanent administrative or political responsibility for the area. Moreover, although some 1,000 or so settlers have moved to Gaza, there is no conceivable way, short of mass expulsion, that Israel can make much of a dent in the demographic picture there. For all these reasons de facto absorption of the Gaza Strip is likely to present clearer political, legal, and ideological choices than is the West Bank. While many Israeli doves have assumed Gaza would automatically go the way of the West Bank, assuming an arrangement with Jordan could be worked out, few on the right in Israel have wanted to draw explicit attention to the especially difficult problems associated with de facto annexation of Gaza.

The Point of No Return

If the debate over the future of the territories has not been comprehensive and systematic, there has been an unmistakable trend toward a clearer focus on the real differences of perception and value that underlay the controversy. Associated with this has been a marked intensification of Israeli political competition. Both these trends are due, in part, to a perception among annexationists and anti-annexationists alike, that there exists a point at which the process of settlement and de facto annexation becomes irreversible--a "point of no return"--and that this point is near.[3] For both camps the perception that a "point of no return" exists, and that political action at the present stage may push the situation past that point or prevent it from being crossed, increases the importance of political struggle. The apocalyptic visions and fears of each side seem to hinge on the course of events in the near term.

A truly hectic rush to confiscate land and establish settlements in the months immediately preceding the 1981 elections reflected the Likud leadership's fear that if the point of no return were not passed, a Labor victory at the polls might forever remove the possibility of securing Jewish sovereignty over the West Bank.[4] Although the pace of settlement slowed

somewhat, it soon quickened again. With the reservoir
of ideologically committed settlers nearly exhausted,
the government developed and rapidly implemented a
blizzard of heavily subsidized real estate developments, apartment complexes, and "build your own home"
projects in the West Bank. Most of the increase in the
number of settlers since June 1981, and most of the increase anticipated over the next several years, is and
will be due to Israelis seeking to take advantage of
housing opportunities in the territories dramatically
better than those available within Israel proper.
Since the end of 1982, those in charge of the settlement process have regularly referred to the figure of
100,000 settlers established in the West Bank as the
point at which annexation of the area will have become
a permanent fact.[5] Although delays stemming in part
from Israel's straightened economic circumstances cast
some doubt upon their projections, schedules published
by the government and settlement authorities indicate
that this goal will be met or surpassed by 1986.[6]

In the Labor party's repeated efforts to break the
Likud's narrow majority in the Knesset, a certain des-
peration has been apparent. Beyond the normally intense desire of any opposition party to unseat the
government, the numerous no-confidence motions sponsored by the Labor party seem to grow out of a frantic
sense that opportunities for preserving Labor Zionism's
vision of the country are rapidly disappearing. Peace
Now's ability in April 1983, to mobilize over 12,000
demonstrators in driving rain and hail to protest, at
the site, the establishment of a settlement overlooking
Nablus, is explained by the perception among anti-
annexation activists that if it is still possible to
stop the de facto annexation process, it will be necessary for at least the Nablus area to be spared intensive Jewish settlement. For some this was seen as the
last possible moment to keep the option of partition
open.[7]

But forever is a long time; and impossible is an
implausible claim when applied to essentially political
processes. Notions of "irreversibility" and "point of
no return" may serve the rhetorical purposes of those
favoring or opposing annexation. They do so not because they correspond with some analytically identifiable and immutable circumstance, but because of their
presumed effect on the calculations and imagination of
participants in the political process. History is
filled with events considered unthinkable by preceding
generations, or even preceding governments. Nations
and states expand, contract, are carved up, divide, and
reunite--all as functions of processes too varied to
permit predictions of <u>permanence</u> to be made with confidence. Strictly speaking there is nothing, short of
the extermination of one of the national claimants to

the land, or the physical destruction of the country
itself, that can justify the nonfigurative use of the
term "irreversible."

Thus, however useful and influential they may be
polemically, from an analytical perspective concepts
such as "irreversibility," the "point of no return,"
and "permanent," must be applied with great care. It
seems less useful to think in such absolute terms, than
to conceive of two distinct thresholds marking trans-
formations in the political meaning of annexation, that
is to say in the scale of political change required for
disengagement. The first such threshold is that point
at which calculations by an Israeli government concerning initiatives that would lead toward disengagement
would be affected more decisively by fears for the survival of parliamentary democracy than by fears of dis-
ruption in the governing coalition. The second, and
more fundamental threshold, is the point at which the
absorption of the territories into the state of Israel
ceases to be problematical for the overwhelming majority of Israelis--i.e., when the question of the future
of these areas is removed from the political agenda,
much as the future of the Western Galilee was removed
from the political agenda by 1950. At this point one
may say, borrowing a much-abused but in this instance
very appropriate term, that the "ideological hegemony"
of annexation has been achieved.[8]

The West Bank and Gaza and the
Breakdown of Israeli Democracy

There is good reason to think that the first
threshold has already been crossed. As Yoval Elitsur
put it in Maariv in November 1983, the unwillingness of
political leaders in Israel to greet the prisoner exchange with the PLO as even a "small step in the right
direction" reflects "a fear--and not only in the Likud
but also, to some extent, in the Alignment--of the internal upheavals that will inevitably result from a
breaking of the political ice."[9] Fear of such upheavals, as opposed to partisan concerns about unfavorable
coalition prospects, has emerged in part because of the
way that the division in Israel over what to do with
the occupied territories relates to other cleavages in
the society.

Many wonder whether intense, explicit, and sustained debate over the future of the territories may be
too explosive and divisive an issue for the survival of
Israeli democracy. Polls show that the major cleavages
in Israeli-Jewish society tend to be congruent--that is
class, ethnic, and religious vs. nonreligious differences tend to correspond with hawkish vs. dovish views
on the territories question. Doves, or those favoring

territorial compromise, tend, proportionately, though
of course not uniformly, to be Ashkenazi, middle- or
upper-middle-class, well-educated, and nonreligious.
Those favoring a hard line toward the Arabs and permanent control of the West Bank and Gaza Strip tend to be
Sephardi, lower class, lacking education, and religious. Polls also very consistently show that the
country is quite evenly divided between those unwilling
to relinquish any part of the West Bank and those willing to trade parts or all of it for peace.
     It is in this context that a number of Israeli
leaders and respected observers have warned that decisive efforts to solve the West Bank problem, or even
continued political debate over it, could push the
country to the brink, or over the brink, of civil war.
In a lengthy open letter to Prime Minister Begin, Israel's leading historian, Yaacov Talmon, pleaded for a
change in government policy toward the West Bank before
it was too late. "Extremism," wrote Talmon in 1980,
"mounts between the two rival parties and within the
Israeli populace. The danger of civil war between
Arabs and Jews, and Jews and fellow Jews, hovers over
us."[10]   A. B. Yehoshua, one of Israel's leading novel-
ists and intellectuals said in an interview in the
spring of 1983 that he did not fear

     a war between brothers...against a background of
     ethnic division, but only in connection with a war
     of rightist groups against the government follow-
     ing another partition of the Land of Israel....
     All the necessary elements are already in place.[11]

Since the grenade attack on a Peace Now demonstration
in February 1983, several Israeli leaders, including
Interior Minister Yosef Burg, (then) President Yitzhak
Navon, Deputy Prime Minister David Levi, and former
Foreign Minister Abba Eban have interpreted the event
as a profound warning of what could materialize in Israel's overheated and polarized political arena. Although these men, and several spokesmen for the Herut
Party have argued that talk of imminent civil war has
been exaggerated, a number of them indicated agreement
with an editorial in Israel's largest circulation newspaper, Yediot Acharonot, that it was time to place
limits on freedoms of speech and assembly in order to
reduce the possibility of violent clashes.[12]
     A number of Israeli analysts have suggested that a
right-wing-supported military takeover of the government could occur should the country face uncontrolled
political turmoil over the territories issue. In early
1981, when it looked as though a Labor party government, one prepared for serious negotiations over the
future of the West Bank, might be coming to power, the
Association of Jewish Local Councils in Judea, Samaria,

and the Gaza District declared that any decision by the
Israeli government to withdraw from integral parts of
the Land of Israel could be treated as "illegal" and
would be resisted.[13] Among those who have recently
warned of extra-legal and/or violent right-wing opposition to territorial concessions are Avraham Achitov,
Israel's secret service chief from 1974 to 1980, Shlomo
Ben-Ami, head of Tel-Aviv University's Department of
history, Shaul Friedlander, winner of the "Israel
Prize" (for history) in 1983, Eliyahu Salpeter, column-
ist for the prestigious newspaper, Haaretz, and Yoram
Peri, former military affairs adviser to Prime Minister
Yitzhak Rabin, and author of a recent study of
political-military relations in Israel.[14] According to
Peri the overlap of religious, ethnic, and political
cleavages in Israeli society makes it

> possible that Israel might at some future time
> face a political crisis much more severe than that
> which has existed since the early seventies, par-
> ticularly having regard to its occupation of the
> territories.... Such a crisis would include the
> fragmentation and polarization of public opinion,
> wider social and political cleavages, and the in-
> ability of the Government to resist political
> groups that deny both the rule of law and the
> binding nature of governmental decisions.[15]

In Peri's view, such a situation would most likely be
triggered by international crisis or external pressure
in which

> the political struggle between the two camps could
> result in impasse and immobility. Given irrecon-
> cilable differences on the fundamental issues of
> Israeli society as an entity, proponents of a
> 'third way' would probably win the day. The army
> might well emerge as a neutral national body
> handed the reins of government by agreement be-
> tween the two rival camps.[16]

Although it is still difficult to imagine an illegal transfer of power or change of regime in Israel,
public attitudes are changing in a direction which
might be supportive of such developments. In polls
conducted after the fatal grenade attack on a Peace Now
demonstration in February 1983, Israelis were asked
whether two leftist-dovish groups: The Committee for
Solidarity with Beir Zayt and Peace Now, and two right-
wing hawkish groups: Meir Kahane's "Kakh" organization
and Gush Emunim, should be outlawed. The results were
as follows:

Group	Percentage Desiring to Outlaw the Group
Committee for Solidarity with Beir Zayt	60
Peace Now	27
Kakh Movement	50
Gush Emunim	22[17]

In another poll of Jewish Israelis conducted in
February 1983, 58 percent of those interviewed thought
that "open criticism of official government positions
in the area of foreign policy and security...should be
banned"; 65 percent felt the mass media's activities
"endangered national interests and should be curtailed"; 20 percent thought it necessary to "change the
political system radically and institute a strong regime of leaders who are not dependent on parties"; and
17 percent "preferred an undemocratic government whose
positions and actions they approved to a democratic one
whose views and actions they opposed."[18]

None of this is meant to suggest that Israeli
democracy is threatened with imminent breakdown. The
point is rather that the concerns of Israelis who con-
template the implications of government initiatives
toward disengagement have shifted from speculation
about coalition survival and the fortunes of particular
parties and politicians, to regime survival and the
integrity of Israel's democratic political culture.[19]
But if the first threshold has thereby been passed with
respect to present or future efforts by the Israeli
political system to disengage itself from the West Bank
and Gaza Strip, the vigor of the debate in the country
over the future of these territories indicates that the
more fundamental second threshold has not yet been
crossed. To be sure, there are relatively few Israelis
that appear capable, publicly at least, of contemplating scenarios for the future of East Jerusalem other
than governance of the city under full Israeli sovereignty. Though this itself makes achievement of an
agreement regarding the disposition of the rest of the
occupied territories much more difficult, the obstacles
to disengagement would be all the greater if the same
cognitive constraints against contemplation of alternatives to the status quo were present with respect to
the future of the West Bank (minus East Jerusalem) and
Gaza.

Indeed, the most basic purpose of the settlement
movement in these areas is to impose just such cognitive constraints. De facto annexation, involving settlements, administrative, legal, and infrastructural
obliteration of the green line, as well as substitution
of "Judea and Samaria" for the "West Bank" in the official lexicon of the government, the educational system,

and in radio and television, are all designed to erase
the green line, not only from the geographical map, but
from the cognitive map of the Israeli public as well.
Disengagement from these territories is to become not
only emotionally unacceptable but, literally, unthinkable. In its first issue of 1984, the editorial board
of Nekuda, a journal published by the association of
Jewish settlements in the West Bank and Gaza, explained
what they thought passage of this second threshold
would entail:

> The central goal of settlement--aside from the
> creation of settlements--is to achieve full inte-
> gration, psychological and real, with the state of
> Israel. Integration is achieved in several ways,
> the first of them, of course, and it is hoped this
> will be accomplished quickly, is the application
> of Israeli law to Judea, Samaria, and Gaza. But
> this is not enough. In order to create the psy-
> chological sense that Judea, Samaria, and Gaza are
> integral parts of the state, Judea, Samaria, and
> Gaza must cease to be problematical areas, espe-
> cially in all that is connected to the ability of
> Jews and Arabs to live side by side.[20]

In addition to the level of unrest prevailing in
the occupied territories, three developments have contributed or will contribute to Israel's passage through
this second threshold: (1) the perception among many
annexationists and antiannexationists in Israel that a
"point of no return" has been passed; (2) a spreading
sense among Arabs that it is either too late to negotiate an acceptable territorial compromise with Israel
given the situation on the ground, or that the Israeli
government's fundamental ideological commitments and
its stance toward the Arab world contradict the minimum
requirements of any peace accord; (3) repeated demonstrations of the inability or unwillingness of the
United States to move Israel toward compromise.
Many Israeli journalists covering events on the
West Bank, and some scholars, are convinced that the
process of settlement and de facto annexation has pro-
ceeded so far on the West Bank that withdrawal has in
fact become impossible.[21] For many Israeli doves,
frustrated at their inability to prevent annexation
from becoming just the sort of fait accompli intended
by the Begin government, this perception has led to a
kind of paralyzing despair about the country's future
and the futility of putting time and effort into anti-
annexationist political activity. Thus, insofar as the
perception takes hold that a point of no return has
been passed, even opponents of annexation will be discouraged from contemplating alternative futures.

Arab acceptance of the idea of a point of no return, and changes in policy that can reasonably be expected to flow from perceptions that it has been reached, will also contribute to processes pushing Israel through the second threshold. Mubarak, Hussein, and West Bank and Gaza moderates such as Elias Freij and Rashad al-Shawa, have repeatedly warned that the point of no return, in terms of Israel's de facto annexation of the territories, is rapidly approaching.[22] On the one hand such perceptions can be seen as contributing to the peace process by encouraging as forthcoming an Arab approach to Israel as possible, before it is too late. Repeated and dramatic warnings of the approach of "midnight" is also a way for Arab leaders to try to heighten the concerns of U.S. policy-makers, who are seen as deterred by domestic political concerns from pushing vigorously toward an Arab-Israeli settlement. But eventually Mubarak, Hussein, and the rest, will have to start taking their own warnings seriously. It will be increasingly difficult for these, or other like-minded Arab leaders, to endorse peace initiatives in the face of Israeli-created facts that they themselves have declared would make peace impossible. As Israeli integration of the West Bank and Gaza proceeds, it will also be harder to convince Arab constituencies less enthusiastic about compromise that the possible payoffs of compromise are likely to exceed the gains of adopting a long-term, more militant posture.

To date, no Arab state that expressed willingness to reach a territorial compromise with Israel in the mid-1970s (Jordan, Egypt, Syria, Saudi Arabia, etc.) has decisively and finally rejected that possibility, although the tenor of Syria's position has hardened. But during and immediately after the Lebanon War a number of Arab leaders expressed their doubts as to whether a peace agreement with Israel was possible any longer.[23] Of course, it has become a commonplace for long-time acquaintances of King Hussein to report his present mood as unprecedentedly depressed about the prospects for peace. The recent split in Fatah, revealing the strength of hard-line sentiment among rank and file guerrillas, can partly be understood as a response to the spreading belief that striving for a territorial compromise with Israel may be no more promising as a strategy for reaching an acceptable status quo than seeking the "liberation of all of Palestine."[24] To the extent that Arabs and especially Palestinians retreat from even ambiguous attempts to seek compromise with Israel, toward slogans and strategies designed for a long-term struggle against Israel's existence, the debate inside of Israel over the question of trading territories for peace will subside. The credibility of the dovish position will be weakened. The argument that there is no one to talk to and nothing to talk about will be strengthened. In turn the absorption of the territories will be transformed from a contingent fact of Israeli political life to an unexamined assumption about the country's future.

One additional factor contributing to this process is the growing perception of American unwillingness or inability to apply significant pressure on Israel. Although President Reagan's initiative of September 1982--which formulated U.S. policy in terms essentially acceptable to moderate Arabs and Labor party doves-- raised expectations that U.S. pressure was about to be applied, the United States did not follow through on the September initiative. Although it is difficult to imagine that withdrawal from the West Bank and Gaza can ever become truly "unthinkable" in Israel as long as virtually the entire world opposes the annexation of those areas, the United States' position and the vigor with which it is advanced are of singular importance in the determination of what is and is not "thinkable" in Israel.

Implications of de facto Annexation of the West Bank and Gaza for Israel's Security and Foreign Policy

Regardless of how far from the second threshold one may judge Israeli society to be, it would be impru- dent for any analyst to expect that the next five to ten years will bring something radically different in the West Bank and Gaza from what is there today. If a Labor party-led government were to emerge in Israel that could act independent of the annexationist reli- gious parties with which Labor has traditionally aligned itself, the debate over the future of the oc- cupied territories would, indeed, intensify beyond the current level. A Jordan-oriented initiative, supported by the United States, could, in that case, result in a phased withdrawal of Israel from most if not all of the territories. But given the internal disarray of the Labor party, the distribution of opinion within the Israeli electorate, the candidates for leadership cur- rently on the horizon, and the chronic irresolution of American policy, this seems much more a ten-to-fifteen year scenario than a one-to-three year possibility.

One other development that could trigger faster- paced change would be prolonged and uncontrollable dis- turbances in the areas. But this seems equally un- likely for an equally long period of time. Not since the end of the IDF's successful campaign in 1970 and 1971 to eliminate armed PLO elements from the Gaza Strip have the inhabitants of the territories posed a serious security problem for Israel. Attempts at sys- tematic violent resistance to the occupation from

inside the West Bank were made in the late 1950s but
were crushed with relatively little effort. Although
waves of street demonstrations and commercial strikes
do occur--whose suppression earns Israel unfavorable
publicity in the Western press--the most significant
security problem facing Israeli authorities in the West
Bank is the protection of civilian traffic from rocks
thrown by Arab youths. While potentially explosive as
a political issue, this, and other personal security
issues relating to the presence of settlers, are not
factors which weigh heavily in Israel's overall security calculations.

In light of the political strength of annexationist forces in Israel, with no prospect of determined
U.S. efforts to change the status quo, and given the
ineffectiveness of local Palestinian opposition, the
continued absorption of the West Bank and Gaza must be
anticipated. This is, de facto, annexation. Its most
serious international consequence will be the inability
of Israel to reach peace or even nonbelligerency agreements with its neighbors to the East. The treaty with
Egypt is likely to hold. But as long as Israel's fundamental approach to the West Bank and Gaza is unchanged, autonomy negotiations with Egypt will not be
resumed and Egypt will permit its relationship with
Israel to wither on the vine.

No matter how slow the process may be, Israel's
relationship with the United States will also suffer.
Combined with the weight of U.S. economic and geo-
political interests in the Arab world, the internal
transformation of Israel from a nation convincingly
characterized as the "only democracy in the Middle
East" to a state struggling to maintain control over a
40 percent minority of subordinated, excluded, and
harassed Arabs, will weaken U.S. support for Israel.
This has already clearly taken place at the elite level
in Washington, and, to a lesser degree, Israel's standing in the eyes of the American public has also deteriorated. Although the domestic political influence of
Israel's friends will continue to prevent this disaf-
fection from being clearly manifest at the policy
level, gradually, and in more and more specific situations, the disjunction of U.S. and Israeli interests
will produce lower levels of American political, economic, and military support for the Jewish state. In
light of the extreme isolation that Israel has experienced in virtually all international arenas since 1977
the alienation of the United States, Israel's last
major economic supporter, international political
patron, and arms supplier, will have severe, if unpredictable, psychological effects.

As long as an Israeli government of the current
ideological complexion remains in power a further consequence of de facto annexation will be a pugnacious

foreign policy--one designed to accomplish four objectives: (1) to demonstrate through the use of armed force the punishment in store for any potential Arab adversary, thereby strengthening the deterrent to war that is Israel's only viable security strategy in the absence of peace; (2) to convince the Arab world, in accordance with the traditional strategy of the "Iron Wall," that Israel's absorption of the territories and its willingness and ability to fight for them are unchangeable facts of Middle Eastern political life; (3) to destroy Arab political and military capabilities that could serve as a basis for pressuring Israel on the issue of the territories' political future; and (4) to maintain a high enough level of tension between Israel and the Arab world that "national security" requirements can continue to be used to justify repression of West Bank and Gaza Arabs, and their exclusion from rights as Israeli residents or citizens.

While the first and second objectives are straightforwardly related to Israel's relations with its Arab neighbors, the importance of the third and fourth relate to both the Jewish and Arab inhabitants of the territories under Israeli jurisdiction. Thus, for example, in regard to Arab-Palestinian political and military capabilities, the Lebanon War was partly fought in order to destroy the credibility of the PLO as a united and representative political force that could exert leverage on Israel through the international community and the Arab world. It was, in other words, precisely the moderating tone of the PLO mainstream in recent years, and the widespread support accorded it by Palestinians in the West Bank and Gaza, that made the PLO so dangerous for the Likud government. Destruction of the PLO was designed not only to eliminate an important player in the international diplomatic arena, but also to so demoralize political activists in the territories that actively cooperative behavior by Arabs there would be easier to elicit. At the same time hatred of Israel among Palestinians for the suffering inflicted during the war would undercut those in the Palestinian camp seeking a compromise political settlement with Israel. Maintaining high levels of tension, on the other hand, relates to the Jewish/Israeli public itself. To implement the kind of policies that will lock the territories into Israel against the will of 1.4 million Arab inhabitants, but without extending equal rights to Arabs, it will be necessary to continue policies of intimidation, confinement, confiscation, and discrimination. Only if high levels of tension are maintained between Israel and the Arab world will national security slogans and justifications be available to neutralize domestic opposition to such policies.

Conclusion

Having crossed the first threshold, described
above, Israel has immured within itself a predicament
fundamentally resistant to amelioration through normal
democratic processes. Powerful, even decisively powerful forces within Israel, are poised to prevent either
the kind of disengagement from the territories that
could lead to peace and a politically controllable Arab
minority in a Jewish state; or the kind of full absorption of the territories and their inhabitants which
could transform the country into one form or another of
a bicommunal democracy. This is one reason political
parties in Israel have been so slow to realign themselves or move beyond slogans designed to elide internal differences. For political entrepreneurs within
the Labor, Liberal, and religious parties the near cer-
tainty of failure deters them from efforts to meet the
issue head on. The intensity and sophistication which
characterize those most involved on each side of the
issue also discourage leaders from attempts to move
toward decisive breakthroughs by camouflaging their
real intentions until they are achieved.
For the foreseeable future, the status quo, which
satisfies no one--not Meir Kahane, the settlers, Peace
Now, the Arab inhabitants of the territories, the Arab
world, or the West--is the most likely scenario. And
Israel waits, torn and embittered by the conflicts and
contradictions de facto annexation has engendered, for
leadership strong enough to move decisively toward disengagement or complete absorption. If the former,
there is no question that dramatic changes in the international constellation of power will be crucial--
shifts in the military balance of power between Israel
and the Arab world that convince Israelis of the necessity of sacrifice for peace, or shifts in United States
foreign policy strong and sustained enough to provide a
"cover" for Israeli leadership to acquiesce in disengagement. In the absence of one or both of these
shifts, a more complete, and, in the medium term, more
stable sort of absorption of the West Bank and Gaza may
be accomplished. That is, instead of recrossing the
first threshold toward disengagement, Israel could pass
the second threshold, toward consensual acceptance of
annexation.
But even if this second threshold were to be
passed, i.e., if the absorption of the West Bank and
Gaza Strip were to be removed from the active agenda of
Israeli politics, the issue might yet reappear someday.
As long as the proportions of Jews and Arabs in the
country are close to what they now are, and as long as
some important support for challenges to the legitimacy
of Jewish sovereignty over the entire area remains in
the international arena, a "separatist" movement is

likely. Focusing on whatever portions of Palestine/the
Land of Israel are most heavily inhabited by Arabs, one
imagines that such a movement would be comprised of
Israeli-Palestinian Arabs, angered at discrimination
and dissatisfied with opportunities for national expression within Israel, along with Jewish-Zionist
purists who might wish to "return" to a more stable,
more homogeneously Jewish state. Should such a movement succeed, in much the same fashion, for example, as
Irish nationalists in league with British liberals succeeded in separating most of Ireland from the United
Kingdom in 1921, an Israeli-binational state would have
proven itself to be a preliminary stage on the long
road to two separate states.

NOTES

1. See interview with Eitan in Bamahane, July 8,
1982; statements by Sharon reported in Foreign Broadcast Information Service, Middle East and Africa Daily
Report (hereafter FBIS), October 28, 1982, p. 11.
2. Speeches transcribed in full in FBIS, October
19, 1982, I1-I14.
3. Meron Benvenisti, "The Turning Point in Israel," The New York Review of Books, October 13, 1983,
pp. 11-16.
4. Yehuda Litani, "West Bank Minefield," Haaretz,
January 16, 1981.
5. See, for example, the statement by Deputy Agriculture Minister Mikha'el Deqel in Yoman Hashavua,
November 12, 1982, reported in FBIS, November 12, 1982,
p. 116.
6. The long-range plan sponsored by the World
Zionist Organization and the Ministry of Agriculture,
titled "A Master Plan for Settlement of Samaria and
Judea: A Develoment Plan for the Area," was approved
by the government in 1983. See reports in FBIS, March
3, 1983, p. 16; FBIS, August 25, 1983, p. 14; and Avraham Dishon, in Yediot Acharonot, August 2, 1983.
More recently the usually exuberant chief of the
Settlement Division of the World Zionist Orgnization,
Mattiyahu Drobles, cut back his predictions. Without
abandoning the goal of 100,000 West Bank settlers by
1986, he predicted (in January 1984) 65,000 West Bank
settlers as early as September 1984, but no later than
June 1985. From ITIM news service, reported in FBIS,
January 24, 1984, p. 13.
Some in the government see the situation in the
West Bank as having already become irreversible. See
remarks by Communications Minister Mordechai Tzippori
to Likud activists, reported in FBIS, December 6, 1982,

p. I14; and Defense Minister Moshe Arens' comments on
Israeli Army radio, reported in FBIS, August 23, 1983,
p. 11.

7. See Amos Elon in Haaretz, April 22, 1983; and
an advertisement sponsored by Peace Now in Haaretz,
April 15, 1983.

8. On the concept of ideological hegemony see Per-
ry Anderson, "The Antinomies of Antonio Gramsci," New
Left Review, No. 100 (November 1976-January 1977),
1-77; and Joseph Femia, "The Gramsci Phenomenon: Some
Reflections," Political Studies, Vol. 27, No. 3 (September 1979), 484-492.

9. Yoval Elitsur, Maariv, November 27, 1983.

10. Yaacov Talmon, "Open Letter to Prime Minister
Begin," in Israleft: Biweekly News Service, #172, June
1980.

11. Interview with A. B. Yehoshua, Haaretz weekly
supplement, April 15, 1983.

12. See Jerusalem Post Weekly Edition, February
13-19, 1983, February 20-26, 1983; Jerusalem Post, editorial, February 11, 1983; Haaretz, February 11, 1983;
Yediot Acharonot, February 18, 1983.

13. See declaration by YESHA in Nekuda, No. 26,
April 3, 1981.

14. Hotam, February 18, 1983; Haaretz, January 23,
1983; Haaretz, April 22, 1983; Davar, August 19, 1983.

15. Yoram Peri, Between Battles and Ballots: Israeli Military in Politics (Cambridge: Cambridge University Press, 1983), p. 284.

16. Ibid., p. 285.

17. According to a poll conducted by Dahaf for
Koteret Rashit, March 9, 1983.

18. Al-Hamishmar, March 20, 1983. Examples of a
spate of articles written by Israelis about the erosion
and possible breakdown of Israeli democracy are
Raphaella Ben-Her Bilski, "Israeli Society at a Turning
Point," Jewish Frontier, Vol. L, no. 3 (March 1983),
5-7; Charles Hoffman, "Israel Democracy's Fragile
Base," Jerusalem Post International Edition, February
27-March 5, 1983; and Moshe Auman, "Removing the
Menace," Jerusalem Post, February 23, 1983.

19. For a discussion of this issue in a related
context see Yael Yishai, "Dissent in Israel: Opinions
on the Lebanon War," Middle East Review, Vol. XVI,
no. 2 (Winter 1983/84), 38-44.

20. Nekuda, January 13, 1984, No. 58, p. 3; my emphasis.

21. See the in-depth interview with Yehuda Litani
and Dani Rubinstein in Al-Hamishmar, April 1, 1984.

22. See for example the interview with King Hussein
given on April 30, 1983, transcribed in FBIS, May 2,
1983, p. F1; Mubarak speech to the United Nations General Assembly, September 28, 1983, transcribed in FBIS,
September 29, 1983, p. D3. For Shawa's opinion see Zvi

Barel, "The List of the Agreed Upon Six," Haaretz, January 20, 1983. For Freij's attitude see the Jerusalem Post, February 15, 1983; March 20, 1983.

23. See the lecture given by Crown Prince Hasan of Jordan to the Army Staff and Command College in Amman in August 1982, reported in FBIS August 18, 1982, p. F1. For Assad's hardened view of the Israeli threat see FBIS June 24, 1983, p. H2 and June 29, 1983, p. H1. At the height of the fighting in Lebanon the Egyptian press contained virulent characterizations of Israeli leaders as incorrigibly belligerent neo-Nazis. See Salamah Ahmad Salamah, "The New Eichmann," in May, June 21, 1982, trans. in FBIS, June 25, 1982, p. D2; and Ismat al-Hawari, "Arabs, Learn Fighting Skills so You will Live," Al-Ahrar, June 21, 1982, trans. in FBIS June 30, 1982, p. D4.

24. See Ian Lustick, "Points of No Return," paper presented to Middle East Studies Association conference, Chicago, November 1983.

7
Some Observations on the Economy in Israel

David I. Fand

American visitors to Israel are confronted by an economic paradox.[1] On the one hand, many things suggest and highlight considerable ability, impressive accomplishments, and extraordinary achievements. On the other hand, many things smack of extraordinary inefficiency--the enormous amount of time required to cash a check, make a deposit, rent a car, or engage in many other similar transactions, by the multiplicity of forms and the queues.

Some of the practices, norms and customs that one sees in the economy and in the marketplace in Israel bewilder someone who was born, and raised, in America. Israeli life is a paradox to an American visitor. It incorporates some of the latest developments that one may find in America, or anywhere else in the world, while at the same time it harbors some antiquated, inefficient, and burdensome bureaucratic procedures and customs that many of the citizens brought with them from their East European background. When viewed in terms of Eastern European economic practices, the nature of the Israeli economy becomes more understandable. Let me summarize some of the main forces that are operating in the contemporary Israeli economy.

The Israeli Economy Before 1973

The period following the 1948 War up to 1973 is one of relatively spectacular economic developments, an average rate of economic growth of about ten percent, inflation rates below ten percent, and rapid growth of per capita income. This period of accelerated economic growth was initiated by high immigration rates and characterized by capital inflow, reparations which added to the available capital, and philanthropy. One might say this was the golden period of Israeli economic development--its growth rates matched those to be found in the most successful economies anywhere in the world.   (See Table 1.)

Table 1
Israeli Economic Performance, 1953-1982 (% p.a.)[2]

Period	1953-1973	1973-1979	1979-1982
Growth rate of real GDP	9.9	3.4	2.3
Growth rate of per capita GDP	6.2	1.0	0.3
Inflation rate (CPI)	7.1	44.9	122.7

The Israeli Economy Since 1973

Since 1973 the Israeli economy has experienced stagnation with very little growth. Inflation rates are high, and rising, reaching triple digits since 1979; productivity and per-capita growth are relatively stagnant; international trade crises occur continually; and the Israeli balance of payments deficit is about $5 billion relative to a GNP of $25 billion. Translating this in comparable U.S. terms, it would imply an American balance of payments deficit of approximately $700 billion. The U.S. now has a staggering trade deficit of $100 billion and a balance of payments deficit of $50 to $70 billion--and this is correctly viewed as truly extraordinary relative to prior U.S. experience.

Israel's Economic Problems Since 1973

It is tempting and natural to blame many of Israel's economic problems on the quantum jump in the resources going into the defense budget, the explosion of oil prices, and the world recession after the OPEC oil price hikes. There can be no doubt that these factors have seriously impaired and hurt the Israeli economy, but it is not correct to put the entire blame for Israel's economic woes on these factors, although they certainly had an important effect.

Politicization of Economic Decision Making

Some part of Israel's economic problem is related to its inappropriate domestic policies. Domestic economic policy in Israel suffers because decision making

is highly politicized. The government is intimately
involved in almost all detailed phases of economic activity and almost all decision making involves some
governmental committees, agencies, or bureaus. In the
1980s taxes averaged over 50 percent of the GNP and
total government revenues were over 60 percent of the
GNP. Government expenditures (current) averaged
79 percent and total government expenditures were approximately 90 percent of the GNP.[3]
     The course of economic affairs may tend to reflect
an equilibrium of different economic interest groups.
Accordingly, this means that major decisions affecting
the course of the Israeli economy reflect a political
equilibrium, which is often achieved at the expense of
economic rationality. One consequence of this approach
to economic policy making is that political maneuvering
to reach economic decisions may foster a cynical attitude toward achievement and innovation. Moreover, an
enterprise may prosper in this environment by obtaining
special favors and privileges, and may not need to in-
novate and develop new and better products.

The Israeli Economy and "Industrial Policy"

     Israel has had an "industrial policy" for many
years, under the "law for the encouragement of capital
investment." Approval by the "Government Center of
Investment" means, in practice, special tax breaks,
special credits, and other benefits. Firms become dependent on governmental aid and lose competitive discipline. The results of this "industrial policy" have
not been helpful to the development of a healthy
economy. As David Levhari notes:

> Israeli industry, for instance, developed under
> what you in this country might call an "industrial
> policy." There was a "Law for the Encouragement
> of Capital Investment," requiring entrepreneurs to
> first submit their investment plans to a bureauc-
> racy, the "Government Center of Investment." Ap-
> proval meant access to all sorts of special tax
> breaks, credit, and other benefits. But this sys-
> tem facilitated uneconomic transactions. Deci-
> sions were not always based on rigorous demon-
> stration [sic] of economic viability, and there
> was always the temptation to submit inflated costs
> in order to get subsidized loans. Firms and in-
> dustries tended to become dependent upon aid and
> lose the competitive discipline necessary to keep
> costs down and productivity up.[4]

Economic Ideology in Israel: The Welfare Economy

Many Israelis grew up with anticapitalist and antimarket attitudes associated with their East European backgrounds. Other Israelis who came from Arab countries had little or no understanding of how a market economy functions. Accordingly, it is not surprising that these attitudes led to a mushrooming of the welfare state in Israel, that the socialist-oriented parties were in the ascendancy in Israel until 1977, and that the public sector grew large relative to the private sector.

Consistent with this pattern, transfer payments in Israel were higher than in most Western countries. Similarly, since 93 percent of the land is owned by the government, most of the credit allocations are handled through government agencies.[5] These developments reflected the approach to economic policy implied in the views of many Israelis who voted then in large numbers for the Labor party.

But the economy clearly was not functioning well after 1973. The combination of increasing defense expenditures and an accelerating welfare state were too much for the Israeli economy. Israel was not in a position to have more guns and more butter. Inflation rates began to accelerate, reaching triple digits in 1979. Growth declined and was averaging less than one-half of the earlier period. Public consumption as a percentage of GNP was rising. The percentage of the labor force in the public sector was rising, as was total taxation. Public dissatisfaction with the relatively inferior economic performance since 1973 was a key factor in the election of the Likud.

The Israeli Economy Since 1977:
A Missing Macroeconomic Policy

When it was elected, the Likud had a platform which advocated a "free economy based on efficiency, initiative, and competition." Unfortunately, there has been very little or no real change in economic policy.

The Likud was really a coalition of two parties: one party, led by Begin, was primarily concerned with national defense and foreign affairs; and another, led by Simcha Ehrlich of the Liberal party, was concerned with developing a market economy in Israel. As it turned out, the Begin wing of the Likud dominated the government's program, and the Liberal party forces under Ehrlich, desirous of a free market approach, did not have much influence on the government's policy, especially since national defense and foreign affairs in the Begin government dominated all other issues.

Economic policy under the Likud seems pretty much a continuation of the kinds of policies that the Israelis had under Labor. When the Likud took office, 28 percent of the labor force was in government; now it is 30 percent. Similarly, transfer payments were 9 percent of the GNP under Labor; now they are 15 percent. Public consumption as a percentage of GNP increased from 11.40 percent in 1974-1977 to 12.7 percent in 1978-81. (See Table 2.)

The international trade crisis, manifested by the extraordinarily large balance of payments deficit, was brought about by the government because it overvalued the shekel--giving the Israelis a 9.8 percent rise in real wages in 1981 and a temporary rise in their standard of living. There is no independent monetary policy. (See Table 2.)

Israeli Public Opinion on Economic Policy

Many Israelis are not well informed about how free markets function. Israelis who came from East European countries and from autocratic Arab countries also do not understand how a free economy that is based on consumer sovereignty allocates resources to produce final goods efficiently. They do not truly understand that competitive institutions and competitive markets are needed in order to realize and achieve high rates of economic growth; nor do they fully understand the connection between economic and political freedom.

Viewed overall, Israeli performance is extraordinary. The Israelis have achieved a relatively good economy and a high standard of living, which is all the more impressive given all the problems they have had to face. The performance up to 1973 was spectacular, but in part this was aided by high immigration, large capital inflow, reparations and philanthropy. The performance since 1973 has been relatively poor, characterized by economic stagnation and triple-digit inflation. While the external environment--resources going into the defense budget, energy prices and the world recession--have much to do with this performance, a lot is due to relatively poor economic policy. These poor policies consist of the politicization of economic decision making, industrial policy that is relatively inefficient, a large welfare economy, an absence of macroeconomic policy that is appropriate for the Israeli condition, and public opinion which does not fully understand the workings of, and the need for, a relatively free economy in order to achieve progress.

Table 2
Israel's Economy: Selected Indicators6

	Inflation Rate	Rate of Change of Real Wages	Rate of Growth of GNP	Public Consumption (% GNP)	% of Labor Force in Public Sector	Total Taxation (% GNP)
1970-73	15.4	3.1	9.4	10.7	24.3	35.7
1974-77	39.6	1.8	2.5	11.4	27.3	44.6
1978-81	95.8	4.3	3.7	12.7	29.6	45.0
1977	42.6	10.6	1.0	12.5	28.0	47.8
1978	48.1	1.5	4.4	12.4	29.2	44.7
1979	111.4	9.5	3.7	13.2	29.5	45.9
1980	132.9	-3.2	2.7	12.6	29.6	44.7
1981	101.4	9.8	4.2	12.5	30.0	44.4

NOTES

1. I have been in Israel in 1968 and again in 1980-81 while on sabbatical leave. The 1968 trip was relatively short, a few weeks, and I was basically a tourist. The purpose of the 1980-81 sabbatical was to study inflation in Israel while serving as a visiting scholar at the Department of Economics at the Hebrew University and at the Bank of Israel.

My knowledge of the Israeli economy is, therefore, very limited and I do not claim to be an expert. However, I have made some efforts to understand the Israeli economy--especially its monetary and foreign exchange policies.

2. Stanley Fischer, "The Economy of Israel," National Bureau of Economic Research, Inc., Working Paper No. 1190, August 1983, p. 1a.

3. Ibid., p. 3.

4. David Levhari, "Israel's Economy: The Challenges Ahead," Manhattan Report on Economic Policy, Vol. III, No. 4 (1983), 3.

5. See Levhari, ibid., p. 4.

6. Manhattan Report on Economic Policy, p. 7.

8
Israeli Economic Policy Under the Likud, 1977–83: A Guide for the Perplexed*

Kenneth A. Stammerman

In late October 1983, the Israeli cabinet was plunged into crisis when the press revealed that Finance Minister Yoram Aridor planned to move the economy onto a dollar standard as a solution to Israel's economic problems. A storm of protest arose from the public, Knesset members, and the cabinet, and Aridor was forced to resign. Prime Minister Shamir, Israel's new head of government, accepted Aridor's resignation and gave the "dollarization" plan a hasty burial.

The purpose of this paper is to review the economic policies of the Israeli Government since the coming to power of the Likud-led coalition in 1977, which ultimately led to Aridor's proposals. The principal players in economic policy making were the finance ministers. Prime Minister Begin took little interest in economic policy and usually endorsed policies established by the ministers. The focus of the paper will be on inflation and the indexation mechanism which has allowed Israelis to live with and, indeed, prosper in spite of triple-digit inflation rates.

The indexation system was not an invention of the Likud. Partial indexing of wages to the consumer price index (CPI) had begun by the late 1960s when inflation rates hit double digits. At that time, some labor contracts provided that wages increase by a percentage based on the CPI recorded in some prior period. Typically, wages were indexed against the CPI on an annual or semiannual basis, much as some major union contracts in the U.S. are adjusted according to the American CPI. As inflation rates stayed high and even increased, savings, most assets and liabilities,

---

*The views expressed herein are solely those of the author and do not necessarily reflect the views of the Department of State or of the U.S. Government.

welfare payments and pensions all became indexed. As
the system spread in a piecemeal manner, distortions
and anomalies arose. Mortgages, for example, were not
indexed until 1980. Since the government was the ultimate mortgage lender, it inadvertantly was the source
of a major transfer of resources from the public sector
to the household sector; unindexed mortgage payments
became nearly worthless after several years of triple-
digit inflation rates. Under the Likud governments,
indexation became more complete, and the most important, or at least the most closely-watched statistic,
was the monthly CPI figure announced on the 15th of the
month.

When the Likud-led coalition took power in May
1977, the economic portfolios were filled by the
center-right Liberal party, and its leader, the late
Simcha Ehrlich, became finance minister. The Likud
itself is a bloc composed of former Prime Minister
Begin's Herut party, the Liberals, and the small La'am
party. The coalition included religious parties, the
Democratic Movement for Change, and other small parties. Ehrlich, a wily politician with a background in
small business, had a free hand in economic policy in
return for Liberal support of Herut's foreign policy
and security positions.

After many years in the political wilderness, the
Liberals had no trained cadre to fill senior positions
at the subcabinet level in the economic ministries.
Indeed, the person filling the senior subcabinet position in the finance ministry for more than a year after
the election, Director General Amiram Sivan, was a
leader of the Labor party Jerusalem branch. However,
the Liberals did have an ideology which meshed well
with the antisocialist outlook of Prime Minister Begin.

The Liberals had long sought to remove what they
saw as the heavy hand of government from the economy.
The Labor party, successor to the labor socialist parties which led Israeli governments since the founding
of the state, had set a major role for government in
the economy. Many major industries were state owned,
the national budget subsidized essential goods and
services, price controls were widespread, and the
finance ministry administered a complex set of foreign
exchange controls. These controls, although often
honored only in the breach, were necessary for maintaining the crawling peg, multiple foreign exchange
rate system through which the government subsidized
exports and penalized imports of various categories.
Finance ministry regulations required, for example,
that exporters had to surrender their foreign exchange
earnings to their commercial banks in Israel. The
banks would then exchange the foreign currency for Israeli pounds according to a formula assigning an exchange rate to various classes of value added in

exports. These regulations gave exporters an incentive
to keep earnings abroad and also encouraged the manipu-
lation of the bureaucracy to have a particular exporter's product placed in the highest exchange rate
class. Importers faced a similar problem in obtaining
letters of credit from commercial banks. Foreign exchange cost more if the government decided that a certain product was a luxury and cost less if it was to be
used to import basic commodities or to serve as an in-
put to export production. It was also illegal to own
foreign currency or, with certain exceptions, bank accounts in foreign currency either in Israel or abroad.
The controls were complex, inefficient, and even the
Labor party officials administering the system realized
that changes were needed.
     Within six months of taking power, Ehrlich decided
to act. In November 1977, he pushed a series of measures through a hastily called cabinet meeting. The
major points of the program, termed the New Economic
Policy, or more simply in Hebrew the economic revolution, were:

- the lifting of most foreign exchange controls;
- the unification and floating of the exchange rate;
- a policy to sell off government-owned
  corporations;
- tightening the budget by slashing subsidies and
  reducing other expenditures in real terms.

     The exchange rate was unified near the free market
rate of the Israeli pound, and Israel's central bank,
the Bank of Israel, announced that it would intervene
in the market only under extraordinary circumstances to
counter destabilizing exchange rate movements. It became apparent after a fairly short time that the foreign exchange regime was the only part of the New Economic Policy that was to be implemented. The Herut
ministers, whose support came from younger Israelis and
Sephardi Jewish voters, were reluctant to allow implementation of budget cuts affecting their constituency,
a problem that continued to plague economic decision
making. In addition, the defense ministry continued to
make ever increasing demands on the budget. It also
became apparent that Israel's private capital market
was simply not large enough to raise the funds needed
to buy out any but the smallest state-owned corporations.
     On the foreign exchange front, however, Ehrlich's
policy proved successful. Contrary to many predictions, there was an immediate and sizable inflow of
foreign currency as controls were lifted. Israelis had
apparently been able to salt away foreign exchange outside the country through the black market. When it
became legal to hold foreign currency, they brought the

funds back to Israel. The central bank had to intervene in the exchange market to prevent a destabilizing
appreciation of the pound, because of the possible effect on exporters' receipts. In the process it soaked
up over $100 million into its holdings of foreign ex-
change reserves in the final two months of 1977.

As the remainder of the New Economic Policy began
floundering, government fiscal policy became expansionary. Unions, seeing the finance minister's weakness in
dealing with demands for defense and welfare spending,
foresaw that expansionary fiscal policy would generate
higher inflation rates. Wage disputes grew as labor
union leaders bargained hard over the 30 percent of
each employee's wage which was not linked to changes in
the CPI. If unions accepted less than was needed in
nominal terms to make up for expected higher future
rates of inflation, real wages would fall. They more
than succeeded, and real wages increased, adding private demand pressures to an expansionary fiscal policy.

A word is necessary here on the financing of the
Israeli state budget. The government sells bonds, col-
lects taxes, borrows at home and abroad, and receives
grants from foreign sources. Insofar as these sources
of funds are not sufficient to finance budget outlays,
the Bank of Israel is required to lend money to the
finance ministry. Usually, foreign funding covers the
foreign currency part of the state budget, but there is
always a sizable deficit in Israeli currency over and
above taxes, grants, and borrowing. The Bank of Israel
simply creates money to fund the remainder of the deficit. This "monetizing" of the budget deficit has
been the major source of Israel's inflation.

Although it was supposedly following a neutral
foreign exchange policy, the Bank of Israel found that
it could not pursue an independent monetary policy,
which it could not effectively accomplish in any case
because of the requirement to fund budget deficits.
When it did try to tighten monetary policy in 1978 and
1979 by imposing credit ceilings on commercial banks,
private borrowers simply borrowed abroad, causing another currency inflow, central bank intervention in the
foreign exchange market, and another runup of foreign
exchange reserves. The Bank eventually decided in 1978
and 1979 that it was unable to determine whether exchange rate movements were destabilizing ex ante without some guide as to what the exchange rate ought to
be. It decided that the best target should be the rate
calculated by purchasing power parity considerations.
That is, the exchange rate should depreciate by the
difference between the Israeli inflation rate and that
of its major trading partners, determined on a trade
weighted basis. Thus, an exporter could remain competitive so long as his average export price increased by
an amount equal to or less than the price increases of

his competitors from the developed world (Israel's export markets are mainly in Europe and North America).
Since his costs were rising by at least a rate matching
Israeli inflation, he had to be able to subtract from
his costs, via the foreign exchange rate, those costs
which were in excess of the increased costs of his competitors, i.e., the foreign inflation rate. In effect,
the Bank of Israel, in setting a target in this manner,
succeeded in indexing the exchange rate.

As the CPI crept up in 1979 to an increase of 78
percent over the previous year's average, Finance Minister Ehrlich came under heavy criticism. Real wages
and foreign exchange reserves were increasing, so Israelis were individually and collectively better off.
Yet they felt worse off because of the psychological
reaction to high inflation rates. Finally, in late
1979 Ehrlich resigned. With his Liberal party in turmoil, and given Ehrlich's reluctance to allow another
Liberal politican to take a senior cabinet portfolio,
Yigael Hurwitz of the small La'am faction of the Likud
became finance minister.

La'am was the remnant of the breakaway Mapai-Rafi
faction which David Ben-Gurion had led out of the Labor
party in the mid-1960s. Although some of the Rafi faction, including Shimon Peres and Moshe Dayan, had eventually returned to Labor, La'am had found a home in the
Likud. Hurwitz, an entrepreneur who specialized in
turning failing businesses around, vowed to run the
economy according to sound business practice. His
strategy was to tighten the budget and cut costs wher-
ever possible.

The watchword under the Hurwitz stewardship of
fiscal policy was "ein li" or "I haven't any." This
remark was his standard reply to the various interest
groups that demanded subsidies or budget increases for
pet ministries. He prodded the cabinet to approve, in
principle, cuts in subsidies, higher interest rates,
and real cuts in budget outlays. His new director general, Yaacov Ne'eman, a dedicated, efficient, and
therefore thoroughly disliked tax expert, cracked down
on tax evasion and closed tax loopholes. On the external side of the economy, Hurwitz obtained the Bank
of Israel's agreement to depreciate the currency faster
than the inflation differential target, to give a boost
to exports. At the outset of his term, the public
favored his measures, since Israelis felt that they had
been living beyond their means, and austerity would be
good for them.

However, two major factors doomed the Hurwitz
policy. The first was the oil shock. Israel returned the Sinai oil fields to Egypt in 1979-80 as
oil prices rose. While the oil import bill increased
considerably, offsetting currency depreciation allowed
the country to pay for the oil without drawing down

foreign exchange reserves. <u>But</u>, the indexing system kept real wages from falling and simply ratcheted the inflation rate higher. In 1980, the CPI increased 131 percent over the average 1979 level. The second factor was the reluctance of other cabinet ministers and their staffs to actually implement the budget cuts decided on in principle. Even though Ezer Weizman resigned over defense budget cuts, the defense ministry itself found ways to deflect major program reductions. The ultimate appeal was to Prime Minister Begin, who paid little attention to economic policy unless the poorer strata of Israeli society or Israel's security appeared threatened. Since these groups would of necessity be affected in an austerity program, Begin's support for the Hurwitz policies waned. Ultimately, with elections looming, Hurwitz had to resign and his major critic within the Likud, Herut's Yoram Aridor, became finance minister.

Yoram Aridor, Israel's first finance minister with an academic background in economics, apparently saw expectations as a key factor in Israeli inflation. He recognized that, in the long run, the balance of payments had to be the main target of economic policy, but also recognized that in the short run inflation could be a target if the balance of payments constraint was not too binding. Knowing that he could not make major changes in the indexing system or impose austerity with elections approaching, he seems to have taken the following view. Unions are able to gain wage increases over and above the rate of inflation in the bargaining over the nonindexed portion of wages because workers and employers alike overestimate future rates of inflation. Unions are also unwilling to accept 100 percent indexing and no wage bargaining, because at a time of rising inflation rates, full indexing to past lower CPI increases never fully compensates workers for higher prices. Therefore, it is necessary to convince wage earners that inflation rates will fall in the future. Unions would then be willing to accept smaller increases in the nonindexed part of wages.

Lowering inflationary expectations would require that the government consistently achieve a lower than expected monthly inflation rate over at least an entire annual wage cycle. During that period, real wages would automatically rise because of indexation mandated wage increases tied to higher past inflation rates. Higher real wages would contribute to larger budget deficits (because the government's wage bill would increase more than tax receipts), higher private consumption, and a larger deficit in the current (goods and services) account of the balance of payments. However, the larger budget deficit would occur only after a lag and would be compensated partially by larger collections of value added taxes on private purchases. Also,

the damage to the balance of payments could be absorbed
for a while by drawdowns of the foreign exchange reserves built up by the balance of payments surpluses
(on reserve account) in the Ehrlich and Hurwitz eras.

Accordingly, Aridor radically changed Israel's
economic policy in early 1981. The cabinet agreed to
his requests to lower the relative prices of basic
goods and government provided services by increasing
subsidies, and to cut tariffs on consumer goods imports. He also changed the exchange rate policy by
depreciating the currency (now called the shekel) at a
rate slower than that called for by differential inflation rates, a reversal of the Hurwitz policy. Imported
goods prices then became relatively cheaper. As upward
adjustments of government controlled prices also
slowed, consumer confidence soared as lower inflation
rates became apparent. In response, Israelis went on a
consumption binge that peaked in the months preceding
the election but which was to last throughout Aridor's
tenure.

Aridor's policy reversal caught the Labor party
completely by surprise. It had figured that it had the
economic issue securely locked away and could simply
point to triple-digit inflation as proof of the Likud's
mismanagement. Labor's election strategy was to harp
on this theme in order to regain some of the traditional support they lost in 1977, while trying to hold
Prime Minister Begin to a draw on security and foreign
policy issues, where the Likud's stance seemed to
appeal to a large part of the electorate. Labor's
shadow finance minister, an academic economist, was no
match for Aridor, and Labor's overconfidence allowed
the Likud to capture the economic issue, a significant
factor in the Likud election victory.

In the second Likud administration, Aridor shored
up his position as economic czar by replacing the Bank
of Israel governor whose term ended and by having the
Bank's deputy governors dismissed. These officials,
all respected technocrats, had kept up a steady stream
of criticism of finance ministry policy. Aridor made
pro forma announcements about the need for budget
discipline, but his target remained the inflation rate.
In 1981, the CPI rose only 117 percent over the average
1980 level.

However, as his second term wore on, it was apparent that Aridor's policy was not seriously affecting
underlying demand pressures. Whether it was because
inflationary expectations were unaffected, or the lag-
ged effect of budget deficits, or a combination of
these factors and the understanding of the Israeli public that the balance of payments constraint would eventually force a change in policy, private consumption
grew rapidly in real terms. Exports grew little in
dollar terms and imports soared as the current account

worsened. The worsening balance of payments picture
made the public suspect that a major depreciation of
the currency was likely. Since the shekel was relatively overvalued in the foreign exchange market, Israelis could cushion the effect of the depreciation by
buying foreign exchange at a rate lower than that which
would exist after the depreciation.

By mid-1983, it was becoming clear that Aridor's
policy was not working. A series of politically damag-
ing strikes, including a doctors' strike, demonstrated
that wage earners did not expect lower inflation rates
and were unwilling to accept lower inflation premiums
in their contracts. Pressure on the balance of payments current account became ever stronger, and it was
only a matter of time until a major correction in the
exchange rate would take place. The choices facing the
government were a return to the Hurwitz policy of fiscal restraint and currency depreciation or a radical
revision of the entire indexing system. Since the
former choice would have been an admission of defeat
and would have required a long-term austerity program
overlapping the election cycle, Aridor decided to seek
a moderately austere domestic economic posture along
with a radical change in the indexing system.

The new plan was reportedly put together by Aridor
and a small group of advisors and was closely held
within the government. The plan drew on the theory of
optimal currency unions and in the first stage would
have substituted dollar linkage for CPI linkage in the
indexation system, following a substantial one-time
depreciation of the shekel. The U.S. dollar would become legal tender alongside the shekel, and would eventually take on most of the functions of domestic money
in Israel. The budget would have to be balanced by
sales of dollar-linked bonds and foreign borrowing or
grants, since the central bank would not be able to
issue dollars or dollar-linked securities. The central
bank would also forfeit any possibility of discretion
in monetary policy; as "dollarization" progressed, the
Israeli economy would essentially become another district of the U.S. Federal Reserve system. In fact,
most discretion in economic policy would be abandoned,
and Israelis would have to follow a set of rules determined by the balance of payments. If Israel consumed
more than it produced, dollars would flow out of the
country, reducing bank reserves and loanable funds, and
reducing economic activity. Interest rates and inflation rates would parallel those in the United States.

It will never be known if Aridor could have made
the system work, since events forced his hand. Whether
devaluation expectations became overwhelming or word of
the dollarization plan leaked, Israelis began to move
out of shekel assets into dollar assets, or simply into
dollar currency. A massive selloff of bank shares hit

the Tel Aviv stock exchange as Israelis sought liquidity to put into dollars. Aridor then went forward with the first part of his plan; he introduced budget cuts and a large depreciation in the exchange rate. With a cabinet crisis already under way because of Prime Minister Begin's resignation, the timing was poor for introducing major changes in economic policy. In the midst of deliberations over Aridor's proposals, an Israeli newspaper published the details of the supposedly tightly held dollarization plan. After a hastily called cabinet meeting, with criticism mounting from Herut's right wing over the loss of sovereignty implied by the plan, Aridor was forced out of the cabinet. Prime Minister Shamir, newly installed in office, referred to the plan as an idea that was never taken seriously.

Aridor was replaced by the fourth finance minister of the Likud era, Yigal Cohen-Orgad. Cohen-Orgad, though of the same party as Aridor, had long criticized his Herut Party colleague. Like Aridor a member of Herut's strong nationalist wing, he heads his own economic consulting firm. The outlines of his policies are unclear, but he apparently is returning to some form of exchange controls, with budget austerity tempered with special assistance to the lower income groups.

What has been the effect of Likud economic policies on the Israeli economy? There are some surprises in the answer, since the popular view of Israel's inflationary economy implicitly uses the analogy of the Weimar Republic hyperinflationary collapse.

One of the more interesting aspects of the economy is the savings rate. Although the press tends to emphasize the complaints of Israeli shoppers that their paychecks never last until the end of the month, Israelis have one of the highest rates of saving of disposable income in the world, at over 25 percent. Since financial assets are linked to the CPI, with a guarantee of a positive real rate of return, Israelis put aside money into pension funds to provide college education for their children, into travel funds (the number of Israelis taking foreign tours has now reached over 600,000 annually, out of a population of 4 million), and until recently, into stock market purchases of gilt-edged bank shares. The important thing is to keep cash and checking account balances small (or negative if banks grant overdraft privileges, as most do).

Another surprising aspect of indexation has been the effect of triple-digit inflation on various socioeconomic groups. The distribution of after tax income tended to remain stable under the Likud or even to narrow as higher income earners were pushed into higher tax brackets even though their real income changes did not justify the higher brackets. Tax brackets were not fully indexed until 1980. Also, the basket of commodities consumed by lower income Israelis tended to contain a large proportion of subsidized items. Thus more discretionary income became available to lower income earners as their real wages increased even faster than that of the average wage earner.

On the balance of payments scene, a floating foreign currency regime, combined with an indexing system which allows the monetary authorities to ignore the effects of a currency depreciation on the level of wages and prices, allows the country to absorb an incipient current account deficit caused, for example, by a hefty negative shift in the terms of trade, without massive unemployment or short-term foreign borrowing. A true free float existed only during the Ehrlich years, and then not consistently. The Hurwitz policy of depreciating the currency at a faster rate than called for by the differential inflation rate guidelines kept the current account deficit lower than it otherwise would have been. Under Aridor's policies, the current account deficit widened, but unrequited transfers, borrowing from the U.S. to finance military purchases, Israel Bond sales, and commercial bank lending allowed his policy to proceed without a rapid drawdown of foreign exchange reserves. The analysis of Israel's balance of payments becomes quite complicated, since there are a number of transfers (e.g., U.S. economic assistance) which enter the central bank's foreign exchange reserve totals without passing through the foreign exchange trading system. What is certain is that foreign exchange reserves, according to IMF data, increased from a little over $1 billion to nearly $4 billion during the Likud administration.

The major drawback to the indexation system is the effect on investment. Since the future rate of inflation is unknowable, the rate of return on private investment cannot be calculated with any degree of confidence. The uncertainty over investment profitability tends to scare off entrepreneurial capital to relatively safe investments such as those favored by the government. Since governments do not make investment decisions as efficiently as those made in the free market, there is a certain loss of efficiency to the economy.

The second major drawback, at least to the government in power, is the so-called reverse money illusion. At a time of high inflation rates, even with real incomes rising, people feel worse off. Uncertainties generated by rapidly changing prices make it difficult to judge on an ex ante basis whether nominal income increases are real. This illusion has often been cited as the cause of unpopularity of Likud economic policy even though full or near full employment has been maintained and real wages and consumption have mounted

throughout the 1977-83 period. It is revealing to
note, however, that when Israelis were given a choice
to throw in their lot with the nonindexed U.S. economy,
they reacted strongly against "dollarization." It
would appear that they did so, not because of a nation-
alistic aversion to losing their own currency--many
Israelis use dollars in day to day business anyway--but
because they understand the benefits of the system.

REFERENCES

Articles

"A Conversation with Dr. Ezra Sadan; Combating Infla-
    tion in Israel." American Enterprise Institute,
    1981.
Crittenden, A. "Israel's Economic Plight." Foreign
    Affairs, Summer 1979.
Fischer, Stanley. "Monetary Policy in Israel." Bank
    of Israel Economic Review, May 1982.

Documents

Bank of Israel Annual Report, 1977 through 1982.
Foreign Economic Trends, Israel, by American Embassy
    Tel Aviv. Published by U.S. Department of
    Commerce, 1977 through 1983.
Income Survey by Israel Central Bureau of Statistics.
    Published in Monthly Bulletin of Statistics, Sup-
    plement, July 1983, in Hebrew.

9
Economic Development in Israel: A Comparative Assessment

Howard Pack

Journalistic accounts of the condition of Israel's economy often raise questions about its "viability" and the extent of its dependence on foreign aid. Such views frequently reveal a poor understanding of simple economics and an unfamiliarity with international statistics that allow Israel's economic performance to be placed within a comparative framework, and permit a balanced assessment of its development. This paper analyzes Israel's past economic achievements and provides salient comparisons with countries in two reference groups: the upper middle income countries as defined by the World Bank in its standard statistical tables and the members of the O.E.C.D., excluding its three poorer members.[1] According to the World Bank rankings Israel stands near the top of the upper middle-income countries.

The Growth of Productive Capacity

Israel's economic development falls into two distinct periods: 1948-73 and post-1973.[2] From independence in 1948 until the late 1950s the major task of the economy was the absorption of the 700,000 immigrants that doubled the population between 1948 and 1955. The numerical and qualitative magnitude of the absorption problem was staggering. Two-thirds of the immigrants were from North Africa and the Middle East and reflected the educational, health, and occupational structures of these countries, while the remaining third, survivors of German concentration camps, required both physical and psychological rehabilitation. Given the immediate need to provide productive employment on a large scale, a development policy was pursued that emphasized the expansion of labor-intensive economic sectors. A considerable effort was made to encourage the agricultural sector and to pursue regionally balanced development, desirable policies only now

beginning to be followed by the majority of poor countries. By the late 1950s most immigrants had been provided with jobs and permanent housing, though it is
likely that their productivity remained below the
national average for a significantly longer period.[3]

A substantial amount of the growth of the 1950s
reflected an expansion in those agricultural and industrial activities that replaced previously imported commodities. Such an "import substitution" phase is typical of the development pattern of almost all poorer
countries. Israel's development path is distinguished
by the relatively short period during which a policy of
import substitution prevailed. Around 1960, the next
necessary stage in Israel's economic evolution became
clear. Given its relative endowments of natural resources, physical capital, and skilled labor, its
future growth, like that of Japan, would have to be
based on the application of an increasingly skilled
labor force to transform imported raw materials into
high valued exports. Expanding industrial exports
would constitute the long run engine of growth to pay
for imports of materials that were not locally available.

Between 1960 and 1970 Israel's merchandise exports
increased by a compound rate of 10.8 percent per year,
among the faster in the world. (See Table 1)

Table 1
Average Annual Growth Rate of Merchandise Exports[4]

	1960-70	1970-81
Israel	10.8%	9.6%
Upper Middle-Income Countries	5.4%	7.0%
O.E.C.D.	8.5%	5.4%

However, merchandise exports consist of all goods,
including unprocessed agricultural produce and minerals
as well as manufactured goods. Given Israel's scarcity
of arable land and mineral deposits, a more salient
measure of export performance is the growth of industrial exports; the sustained growth of the economy depends on success in this area. Although the increase
of industrial exports, beginning from a low base, was
very rapid in the 1960s, the total had reached only
$375 million by 1972. As can be seen in Table 2,
however, growth since then has been extraordinarily
fast; in the decade 1972-82 the compound growth rate
was 25 percent.[5]

Table 2
Industrial Exports[6]

	Millions of Dollars		Annual Growth Rate (%)
	1972	1982	1972-82
(1) Chemicals	43	648	31
(2) Metal Products	37	515	30
(3) Machinery	9	112	29
(4) Electrical and Electronic Equipment	19	466	38
(5) Transport Equipment	7	440	51
(6) High Technology	116	2181	34
(7) Other Industrial Exports	259	1351	18
(8) Total Industrial Exports	375	3532	25
(9) High Technology Share (6)/(9)	.31	.62	

An increasing share of industrial exports consisted of products in sectors such as chemicals, metal products, machinery, electronics and transport equipment whose design requires considerable research and development and whose production involves skilled labor; such products often earn the accolade of high technology though there is a considerable variance in the "high technology" component of the products manufactured by these sectors.[7] Nevertheless, for conciseness these will be referred to as high technology sectors. Their average rate of growth in 1972-82 was 34 percent per annum, in contrast to the still rapid but slower growth of other industrial exports of 18 percent per annum. These growth rates are among the highest in the world and have resulted in a rapid restructuring of the industrial sector as exports have become an increasingly large component of total industrial production. By the early 1980s exports in the high technology sectors accounted for 6 percent of total industrial exports and Israeli companies such as Elscint and Scitex had achieved international recognition for their product innovations.[8]

While exports provide the means for sustaining growth, ultimately the most important measure of the success of an economy is its growth in real or constant price gross national product per capita. Income per capita grew at an annual rate of 4.5 percent during the

period 1950-75, one of the half-dozen highest rates in
the world excluding the OPEC countries. (Table 3)

Table 3
Rate of Growth of Gross National Product per Capita[9]

	1950-75 (%)	1960-70 (%)	1970-81 (%)
Israel	4.5	4.6	1.4
Upper Middle-Income Countries	3.4	3.9	3.4
O.E.C.D.	3.2	4.0	2.3

Moreover, unlike some other rapidly growing countries, Israel did not experience any significant increase in the inequality of its income distribution
through the mid-1960s; data in the period since then
are not sufficiently comprehensive to permit such general statements. Indeed, in international comparisons,
its income distribution was among the most egalitarian,
a result largely attributable to the high employment
strategy and the emphasis on sectoral and regional balance.[10]

The growth in per capita income since 1950 has
been accompanied by a significant transformation of the
structure of the economy, manufacturing's share of GNP
and total employment increasing, that of agriculture
declining. With a small agricultural sector and a
large service sector, Israel is indistinguishable from
the O.E.C.D. countries. (Table 4)

The dreams of visionary socialists about an agri-
culturally-based economy and the transcendent importance of agricultural labor disappear befoer the inex-
orable logic of Engel's Law and comparative advantage.[11]
Nevertheless, the legacy of these early "planners" was
the emphasis on fostering the agricultural sector; by
contrast, the conscious neglect and exploitation of
agriculture has been a major source of the failure of
economic development efforts in many countries in the
postwar period.[12]

The two OPEC price increases and the ensuing
world-wide recession and inflation since 1973 slowed
Israel's growth, as they did that of most other countries (Table 3). For the years 1970-81, Israel's
growth in per capita income declined to 1.4 percent per
annum (Table 3), slower than that of both the O.E.C.D.
and the upper middle-income countries. Much of the
decrease in Israel's aggregate rate of growth is attributable to a decline in the growth of productivity,

Table 4
The Share of GNP Originating in:[13]

	Agriculture		Industry (of which):		Manufacturing		Services	
	1960	1981	1960	1981	1960	1981	1960	1981
Israel	11	5	32	36	23	26	57	59
Upper Middle-Income LDCs	18	10	33	39	23	24	49	51
O.E.C.D. Countries	6	3	40	36	30	25	54	61

production per unit of labor and capital.[14] A similar
reduction in other countries including the United
States has been the subject of intensive research that
has yielded approximately as many explanations as there
are investigators of the phenomenon. The important
point to emphasize is that the slowing of Israeli
growth, viewed in an international context, is far from
atypical. A reasonable conjecture is that Israel's
growth rate will accelerate along with that of the
O.E.C.D. and richer LDCs, and that proper economic
policies, including the encouragement of research and
development, may well allow the rise in Israel's income
to exceed that of its peers.[15]

Demand Management

Success in increasing productive capacity rarely
captures headlines: the accumulation of managerial and
labor skills, small adaptations of equipment and production processes, improved inventory control and other
sources of growth develop slowly, and are usually
noticed only in retrospect. In contrast, the failure
to manage aggregate demand correctly may result in inflation or balance of payments problems, phenomena that
can be summarized by one or two dramatic numbers. Not
surprisingly, it is precisely in these two dimensions
that Israel's economic performance, like that of other
countries, has received most attention, while its impressive supply side achievement has been largely
ignored.

Inflation

Economic growth accompanied by a stable price
level and a balance in international payments requires
a complex combination of appropriate budgetary, monetary, and exchange rate policies to insure that the
growth of domestic demand does not exceed supply, and
that the demand for imports is matched by exports. In
attaining these goals, narrow economic difficulties
pale beside the political ones. Among the changes
necessary to improve the balance of payments, for example, are governmentally induced decreases in some
combination of household consumption, public sector
spending, and private investment. In Israel as in
other countries, each category of expenditure has a
powerful constituency fighting for its maintenance.
Similarly, recent debate about the loan conditions imposed by the International Monetary Fund results from
the perception of recipient governments that the stipu-
lated reductions are politically unacceptable. Though
the balance of payments difficulties of Israel and

other countries is soluble in technical economic terms,
the genius to construct political coalitions permitting
the appropriate policy package to be implemented is, to
be charitable, not widely available.

Israel's policy makers thus encounter a dilemma
similar to that faced in other countries, though their
problem is more severe. This has not always been the
case. As can be seen in Table 5, Israel's inflation
rate in the 1960s was a relatively modest 6.2 percent
per annum.

Table 5
Average Annual Rate of Inflation*[16]

	1960-70	1970-81	1980-81	1981-82
Israel	6.2	45.5	127	121
Upper Middle-Income Countries	3.0	18.6	-	-
O.E.C.D.	4.3	9.9	-	-

*Rate of increase of gross domestic product implicit
 price deflator.

In the 1970s the inflation rate rose in steps,
accelerating after the Yom Kippur War in 1973 and then
again in 1977, reaching triple digits in 1979 with no
decline in the following years.[17] As in all infla-
tions, part of the stimulus arises from excess demand,
part from cost increases that are beyond the control of
the economy. Most obviously the rapid growth in oil
prices affected Israel, but so did the very large increases in the prices of other commodities that must be
imported. However, the fact that other upper middle-
income countries experienced slower inflation, on the
average, suggests that some factors specific to Israel
were of importance, particularly in the acceleration
since 1977.

Most observers agree that the major factor operating to aggravate the inflation resulting from supply
shocks has been the unusually large government deficit
and the fact that much of this is financed by the issu-
ance of money, rather than by other noninflationary
means.

Because of the large defense outlays abroad, along
with external financing of some of these, the total
budget inclusive of foreign operations is of limited
usefulness in analyzing the impact of the government on

the inflation process; it is necessary to focus on the
net effect of the government sector on demand within
the domestic economy. Table 6 shows both the domestic
deficit and domestic defense spending.

Table 6
Government Domestic Deficits and Defense Spending[18]

	(1)	Percentage of GNP (2)	(3)
	Domestic Deficit	Domestic Defense Spending	Government Non-Defense Spending Taxes (1)-(2)
1964-66	3	6	-3
1967	6	10	-4
1968-72	4	13	-9
1973-74	11	16	-5
1979	18	14	4
1980	18	14	4
1981	21	15	6
1982	13	16	-3

The levels of both have increased over time,
though the domestic deficit has risen more. It has
been argued convincingly that the official statistics
understate the true domestic costs of defense, for example, by not including the loss in civilian output
engendered by considerable reserve duties.[19] It is
clear that the burden of defense spending, even with
the foreign exchange component partly paid for by U.S.
aid, imparts an inflationary potential to the government budget that can only be offset by restrictiveness
in civilian budgetary outlays and by a high level of
net taxation (taxes minus subsidies and transfer payments). A noninflationary fiscal policy requires the
net tax and expenditure structure to yield no deficit
as the economy approaches full employment.

Unfortunately, fiscal policy has not followed this
guideline. Large government deficits have resulted
from growth in civilian expenditures, reflecting both
an increase in total government nondefense employment
and in real wages in the public sector.[20] Simultaneously, a program of subsidies, introduced partly to
mitigate some of the distorting effects of inflation,
has offset a large part of the very high gross tax receipts. Given the already high ratio of taxes to income, further tax increases are not realistic without
severely discouraging work incentives or encouraging

tax avoidance. Facing these constraints, the government must decrease the rate of growth of its nondefense spending and must reduce subsidies. Both measures would have unpleasant effects on those directly affected, but some small hardships are inevitable if government sources of inflationary demand are to be reduced.

The Balance of Payments

While inflation, partly attributable to the failure of government to reduce its deficit, has been one major concern for the Israeli economy, the other major dilemma has been a persistent excess of imports of goods and services above exports, loosely called the balance of payments problem. In 1982 the ratio of imports minus exports (the trade deficit) to gross national product was 21 percent, not atypical for recent years. This ratio is somewhat lower than that which prevailed in the early 1960s but is fairly typical for the entire period since the founding of the state. Although the ratio has remained roughly constant, the absolute magnitude has increased considerably with the growth in GNP: thus the import surplus was around a half billion dollars in the middle 1960s and in 1982 reached $4.7 billion.

Should this trade imbalance in fact constitute a source of worry? Assume for the moment that sufficient foreign funds could be obtained, without political conditions, to finance it and that none of the additional real resources were used for defense. In this case the desirability of an import surplus depends on the net gains to the economy that can be obtained as a result of it. For example, if the import surplus were entirely devoted to augmenting the level of investment, the rate of return on investment must be compared with the interest cost incurred to finance the deficit. Just as a household may improve its financial position by obtaining a 10 percent mortgage to finance a home whose price appreciates by 15 percent per year, an economy may benefit from an analogous transaction. It could be argued that until the Six Day War in 1967 the assumptions just used were approximately satisfied and that the recurrent import surplus reflected sensible economic policy, though some of the expectations it bred may have sown the seeds for later problems.

In recent years, however, the realism of the preceding assumptions has diminished. A considerable part of the import surplus represents direct outlays on military hardware and indirect defense imports (steel used in tanks that are locally manufactured). Thus, rather than improving productive capacity, broadly defined, some substantial fraction of imports is deflected to nonproductive uses. Moreover, in recent years, as noted earlier, the rate of productivity growth has slowed, and there is likely to have been a corresponding decline in the rate of return on invest- ment. With respect to the supply of funds, there have been two changes: (1) the growing importance of offi- cial aid from the U.S. Government and the fact that a considerable part of this aid is in the form of loans rather than grants; (2) a growth in intermediate and long-term commercial borrowing. Even where interest rates are low, it is not optimal to borrow unless the return on the marginal investment made possible exceeds the interest cost. Given the changes in conditions just noted, it is no longer clear that this condition is satisfied.

Another difference from the earlier period is the possibility that political conditions will be attached to additional U.S. aid, a loss in sovereignty that few governments are willing to accept. Thus, whatever the economic desirability of import surpluses in an earlier time, it is clear that these conditions are likely to have been sufficiently altered to warrant a move toward a significant reduction.

To put the balance of payments problem into per- spective it is helpful to distinguish between civilian and military components. Table 7 shows that in recent years direct defense imports have constituted one-third to one-half of the excess of imports of goods and serv- ices over exports.

The civilian component was about $3.2 billion in 1982. Assume that a policy decision had been made to eliminate this completely by reducing private consump- tion by an equivalent amount. Such a decision would have resulted in a rough decline in private consumption of 20 percent.[21] While this appears to be of enormous magnitude, total private consumption increased in real terms by 19 percent between 1980 and 1982; thus, even a drastic measure to eliminate the nondefense component of the import surplus would have reduced total private consumption in 1982 to the level of 1980.[22] There are few residents in Israel who would claim that the 1980 standard of living was unacceptably low. On the con- trary, per capita real consumption grew by 3.4 percent per year between 1967 and 1981. Clearly the policy dilemma is a political and psychological one, espe- cially in view of the fact that such a dramatic one- shot change in policy would hardly be necessary; a phased reduction in private consumption and in public nondefense spending would sharply attenuate the re- quired short-term adjustment.

Even if the above policy had been adopted in 1982, it would have left a $1.5 billion deficit to be covered. However, private sector receipts of uni- lateral transfers totalled $1.07 billion, which would

Table 7
Imports and Consumption[23]

		1980	1981	1982
(1)	Total Import Surplus (millions of dollars) Percent of Total	3,776 (100)	4,329 (100)	4,720 (100)
(2)	Direct Defense (millions of dollars) Percent of Total	1,692 (45)	2,190 (51)	1,552 (33)
(3)	Non-Defense Import Surplus (millions of dollars) Percent of Total	2,084 (55)	2,139 (49)	3,168 (67)
(4)	Civilian Import Surplus (millions of shekels)	6,897	18,326	72,678
(5)	Private Consumption (millions of shekels)	63,260	153,269	356,126
(6)	(4)/(5)	.11	.12	.20

have left only about $.5 billion to be covered by a combination of U.S. aid and other sources of international funds. Given Israel's GNP of $22 billion and exports of $10.5 billion, commercial lenders would have readily filled the gap.

Similar calculations of the magnitude of the required policy change hold as of spring 1984 and have indeed applied for almost Israel's entire economic history. Put succinctly, at any point in the past thirty years a decline in consumption to the level that held two or three years earlier would have solved Israel's balance of payments problem. Why then have the required policies not been implemented, particularly as concern has increasingly been expressed about possible political conditions imposed on future aid as well as the handicap an apparently fragile economy imparts in international relations? The same question can be posed about why neither the President nor Congress acted in 1983-84 to reduce record budgetary and foreign trade deficits as the United States economy rapidly approached full employment. Both cases represent an effort to avoid the adverse political consequences stemming from the required restrictive policies: in neither Israel nor the U.S. has the failure to act been attributable to an absence of professional advice, though it has been received with some skepticism.[24]

Not only has there been an unwillingness to follow appropriate policy recommendations, but on several occasions the opposite policies have been pursued to increase electoral prospects. During 1981, Finance Minister Yoram Aridor reduced import duties on several luxury imports, thus conforming to policies of other governments that have recently become the focus of numerous studies on the "political business cycle."[25]

The necessary policy package in light of the preceding is a reduction in government nondefense spending on goods and services, a decrease in its transfer payments and subsidies, and efforts to decrease household consumption. Part of the latter should be engendered by a decline in subsidies and transfers, while holding taxes at their current levels. In addition, a decline in real wages, brought about by eliminating the current policy of linking wages to the inflation rate, would also contribute to the required reduction in household disposable income. However, any measure to decrease household income will be intensely opposed, particularly if the method is to rely partly on wage erosion through inflation. The latter path requires the willingness of Histadrut, the national trade union, and its individual members, to forego a device that has considerable historical sanction and is widely viewed as a mechanism not only to maintain real incomes but to prevent any significant redistribution as a result of inflation.

As in many other countries, including the United States after the price shocks of the 1970s, no group is keen on accepting the inevitable (at a national level) reduction in the real standard of living. Moreover, highly publicized nationwide wage bargaining in Israel precludes any group suffering from money illusion. Many economies currently face similar problems--indeed the international debt crisis of 1983 and 1984 can be understood largely as the unwillingness of governments to impose a reduction in living standards at the behest of external creditors including the International Monetary Fund. Some governments such as Argentina's seem to be willing to accept the consequences of default rather than implement the necessary cutbacks. While Israel does not face such an unpleasant choice in the short run, limits on its long-run borrowing ability will inevitably force adoption of the necessary changes if corrective policies are not undertaken. A voluntary and gradual approach is much to be preferred, though at present it appears to be politically unattainable.

Despite potential long-term problems, at present levels Israel's net foreign debt does not present a serious problem.[26] At the end of 1982 it was $15.5 billion and the debt service (interest and principal repayment) was 25 percent of exports.[27] This compared to an average of 15.4 percent for all upper middle-

income countries, and considerably higher ratios in
such countries as Algeria, Brazil, and Mexico.
Moreover, as the world economy comes out of its recent
recession, Israel's exports are likely to resume their
rapid growth, reducing the burden of debt service.

Conclusions

Israel is one of the few countries to have developed from a low-income, resource-poor country to a
highly developed one in the post-World War II period.
It has absorbed an enormous number of immigrants into
productive employment and simultaneously attained developed country norms in most noneconomic dimensions in
which national well-being is measured such as the in-
fant mortality rate, life expectancy, and education
levels. The two areas in which economic performance
has been deficient have been price stability and the
foreign trade deficit.
The extraordinary burden of defense has contributed to the difficulties in both areas. For comparison, one need only think of the problems the U.S.
would face if its defense outlays increased from 5 to
30 percent of gross national product. Nevertheless,
despite the continuation of defense outlays at their
current level, the balance of trade could be rectified
by a reduction in the level of private consumption that
would not impose severe hardship on Israelis--though
they would obviously be happier without such a policy.
While the rate of inflation would also probably respond
to policies that reduce private consumption and public
nondefense spending, a significant reduction will not
be easy to achieve in a relatively short period of
time. While a slowing of inflation is desirable in
order to release the human and material resources currently employed to cope with it, its main adverse effect probably stems from alterations that it may engender in the distribution of income. Such changes can
be avoided by continuing the current structure of linking arrangements in which all income sources are linked
to a price index, but reducing the degree of linkage to
less than one hundred percent.
While it would be foolish to ignore some of the
serious errors in macroeconomic policy that have been
committed by Israeli policy makers in recent years, it
is important to remember that the policies and their
adverse impact are reversible. Like the countries of
East Asia, Israel's ability to expand total production
and exports bodes well for the future. Unlike the
high-debt, high-inflation countries of Latin America,
Israel is not approaching a threshold at which its
ability to meet external obligations is questionable.
More rapid growth in the world economy combined with

moderately competent economic policy should quickly at-
tenuate the problems currently being encountered by
Israel though it is not clear that a return to the
rapid growth of its first two decades can be expected.

Acknowledgment

This is an expanded and revised version of a paper
published in American Policy in the Middle East: Where
Do We Go From Here? (New York: The Josephson Research
Foundation, 1983). Published by permission of the
Josephson Research Foundation.

NOTES

1. Greece and Portugal are members of the middle-
income group and Turkey is assigned to the low middle-
income group of countries.
2. A detailed analysis of the period 1948 to 1967
is given in H. Pack, Structural Change and Economic
Policy in Israel (New Haven: Yale University Press,
1971).
3. Ibid., pp. 25-28.
4. Source: World Development Report, 1983
(Washington, The World Bank, 1983), Appendix Table 9.
Upper middle-income countries comprise the richest
group of less developed countries according to the
World Bank rankings. Israel is among the countries at
the higher end of this group. "O.E.C.D." excludes the
three poorer members, Greece, Turkey, and Portugal, of
O.E.C.D. members.
5. This is the rate of growth of the value of industrial exports excluding polished diamonds.
6. Source: Bank of Israel, Annual Report, 1973,
Table IX-9; Bank of Israel, Annual Report, 1982,
Table VII A-5.
7. Although not all of the commodities in each
sector embody large amounts of research or highly
educated labor, it is unlikely that an increasing share
of output in these branches in fact represents the high
technology end of the product spectrum.
8. Table 2, line 9.
9. Source: D. Morawetz, Twenty-Five Years of Economic Development 1950 to 1975 (Washington, The World
Bank, 1977), Tables 1, 4; and World Development Report,
1983, Appendix Tables 2, 19.
10. For an analysis of the sources and consequences
of the relatively equal distribution see H. Pack, "Income Distribution and Economic Development: The Case

of Israel," in M. Curtis and M. Chertoff, <u>Israel:</u> <u>Social Structure and Change</u> (New Brunswick, Transaction Books, 1973), and Pack, op. cit., Chapter 8.

11. Engel's Law roughly states that the share of income accounted for by the agricultural sector will decline as per capita income increases, largely as a result of limited demand for agricultural products as incomes increase. Comparative advantage implies that a country will export goods whose production requires productive inputs with which the country is relatively liberally endowed. In Israel, both "laws" militate in favor of the production of goods requiring large amounts of skilled labor and capital.

12. For a thorough account see M. Lipton, <u>Why Poor</u> <u>People Stay Poor</u> (Cambridge: Harvard University Press, 1977).

13. Source: <u>World Development Report 1983</u> (Washington, The World Bank, 1983), Appendix Table 3.

14. A careful analysis of the behavior of productivity in Israel in recent years is provided by J. Metzer, "The Slowdown of Economic Growth in Israel: A Passing Phase or the End of the Big Spurt" (Jerusalem: The Maurice Falk Institute for Economic Research in Israel, 1983).

15. A thorough discussion of public policy towards research in Israel is given by M. Teubal, "The Industrial Technology Promotion System in Israel: Some Analytical Questions" (Jerusalem: The Maurice Falk Institute for Economic Research in Israel, 1983).

16. Source: <u>World Development Report</u>, 1983 (Washington, The World Bank, 1983) Table 1; <u>Bank of Israel</u> <u>Annual Report, 1982</u>, Table 1.1.

17. An attempt to explain the acceleration of inflation and other dimensions of Israel's recent macroeconomic performance is given in S. Fischer, "The Economy of Israel," National Bureau of Economic Research Working Paper No. 1190, 1983.

18. The figures in the two columns do not always pertain to exactly the same time period. Source: <u>Bank</u> <u>of Israel Annual Report, 1982</u>, Tables V-1, VA-4.

19. E. Berglas, "Defense and the Economy: The Israeli Experience" (Jerusalem: The Falk Institute for Economic Research in Israel, 1983).

20. For empirical evidence on these see Bank of Israel, <u>Annual Report</u>, 1982, Tables I.1, IV-2 and IVA-9 and the discussion in Chapters IV and V.

21. Rough, because a complete analysis requires the use of a fully specified econometric macroeconomic model of the Israeli economy plus the use of an input-output table. The calculation in the text implies that the entire reduction in consumption consists of final imported consumer goods.

22. Given a 3.7 percent growth in population over these years, per capita consumption would actually have

been roughly this much lower, but the major thrust of the calculation stands.

23. Sources: Bank of Israel, Annual Report, 1982, Tables VII-3 and Table II-1.

24. Among the earliest published statements about the need to move towards a reduction in budgetary and trade deficits is Don Patinkin's The Israel Economy: The First Decade (Jerusalem: The Falk Project for Economic Research in Israel, 1960). Such advice has continued to be proffered by both academic and government economists. For excellent examples of the latter, see recent volumes of the annual Bank of Israel report. One reason that may account for politicians' skepticism about the usefulness of professional economic opinion may be the assertions by British economic missions in the 1930s that the economic absorptive capacity of what was then Palestine had reached a limit and no additional immigrants could be productively employed within an economy with limited natural resources--conspicuously bad forecasts.

25. W. Nordhaus, "The Political Business Cycle," Review of Economic Studies, April 1974; and D. A. Hibbs and H. Fasbender, eds., Contemporary Political Economy (Amsterdam: North Holland Publishing Co., 1981).

26. External debt minus foreign assets owned by Israelis.

27. Bank of Israel, Annual Report, 1982, Table VII A-15.

28. World Development Report, 1983 (Washington: The World Bank, 1983), Appendix Table 16. These ratios represent service on gross debt, net debt not being reported.

About the Contributors

MYRON J. ARONOFF is professor of political science at
Rutgers University. Before joining the faculty of
Rutgers University, Professor Aronoff taught at Tel
Aviv University for eight years. He was a Fellow of
the Netherlands Institute for Advanced Studies, and has
held grants and fellowships from the Social Science
Research Council of the United Kingdom, the Ford Foundation, and the Joint Committee on the Near and Middle
East of the American Council of Learned Societies and
the Social Science Research Council. Dr. Aronoff is
the author of Frontiertown: The Politics of Community
Building in Israel, and Power and Ritual in the Israel
Labor Party. He has edited Freedom and Constraint: A
Memorial Tribute to Max Gluckman and the first four
volumes of Political Anthropology, the most recent volume of which is entitled Cross Currents in Israeli Culture and Politics. Professor Aronoff is currently
writing a book titled Israeli Visions and Divisions:
Cultural Change and Political Conflict.

DAVID I. FAND is professor of economics at Wayne State
University. He earned a Ph.D. in economics at the University of Chicago, has taught at the Carnegie Institute of Technology, Brown University and the University
of Chicago. He has been a visiting scholar at Jagel-
lonian University in Cracow, Poland, at Hebrew University in Jerusalem and at the University of Tokyo. A
consultant to government and business, Dr. Fand is a
member of the advisory boards of several scholarly economic journals.

JERROLD D. GREEN is a member of the Department of Political Science and the Center for Near Eastern and
North African Studies at the University of Michigan.
He is the author of Revolution in Iran: The Politics
of Countermobilization as well as articles in such
forums as Comparative Politics, Middle East Insight,
and the Political Anthropology Yearbook. Green

135

recently spent a year as a Fulbright professor at Cairo
University and visited Israel several times where he
lectured at the Hebrew University as well as at Haifa
and Tel Aviv universities.

IAN S. LUSTICK is associate professor of government at
Dartmouth College. Dr. Lustick obtained a B.A. from
Brandeis University and an M.A. and Ph.D. from the University of California at Berkeley. An associate professor of government at Dartmouth College, Dr. Lustick
has worked in the State Department and served as a consultant to private industry. He is the author of Arabs
in the Jewish State: Israel's Control of a National
Minority and Israel and Jordan: The Implications of an
Adversarial Partnership, as well as numerous journal
articles.

HOWARD PACK is professor of economics at Swarthmore
College. Before joining the Swarthmore faculty in
1970, Dr. Pack was assistant professor of economics at
Yale. He has been a research associate at the University of Pennsylvania, the Institute of Development
Studies (Nairobi) and the Hebrew University in Jerusalem. He has served as a consultant on development to a
variety of international organizations, including the
World Bank and the United Nations Conference on Trade
and Development. He has written widely on Israeli economic development; his publications include Structural
Change and Economic Policy in Israel.

BERNARD REICH is professor of political science and
international affairs at George Washington University
in Washington, D.C. Dr. Reich was a Fulbright Research
Scholar in Egypt in 1965 and a National Science Foundation Postdoctoral Fellow in Israel in 1971-72. He has
served as a consultant to various U.S. government agencies. Among his numerous publications are Quest for
Peace: United States-Israel Relations and the Arab-
Israel Conflict and The United States and Israel: Influence in the Special Relationship.

GARY S. SCHIFF is president and professor of Middle
East studies at Gratz College. A graduate of Yeshiva
University, Dr. Schiff went on to obtain M.A. and Ph.D.
degrees from Columbia University. Prior to assuming
his current position, he worked for the Academy for
Educational Development, a nonprofit, educational consulting and planning corporation. Dr. Schiff has
served as director of Middle East and Energy Affairs
for the National Jewish Community Relations Advisory
Council. He has taught at the City University of New
York and at Yeshiva University in New York. Among his
publications are Tradition and Politics: The Religious
Parties of Israel, "Religion and State Under Begin," in

The Canadian Zionist (November 1977) and "The Politics of Fertility Policy in Israel," in Paul Ritterband, ed., Modern Jewish Fertility.

ZEEV SCHIFF is defense editor of Ha'aretz and a senior associate of the Carnegie Endowment for International Peace. Mr. Schiff, who joined the staff of Ha'aretz prior to the 1956 Sinai campaign, has been defense editor since 1970. He is currently on leave as a senior associate with the Carnegie Endowment. He is the author of numerous books and articles on Israeli security and defense. His latest book, on the war in Lebanon, will be published in the fall of 1984. A graduate of Tel Aviv University, Mr. Schiff won the Israeli Editors' Prize as Journalist-of-the-Year in 1983 for his coverage of Lebanon, and the Sokolov Prize in 1974.

KENNETH A. STAMMERMAN is deputy coordinator for economic and commercial studies in the Foreign Service Institute. Mr. Stammerman began his foreign service career in 1967. After serving in Tel Aviv as commercial and consular officer, he was assigned as an economic/commercial officer to Manila in 1970. He later served on the international staff of the OECD in Paris before returning to Tel Aviv, where he was the embassy financial economist from 1977 to 1981. On completion of his tour, he was assigned as economic officer in the Office of Egyptian Affairs in the Department of State.